Finding *Me*

in the Midst of It All

RUTH GOLD

WESTBOW
PRESS®
A DIVISION OF THOMAS NELSON
& ZONDERVAN

Scripture quotations marked AMP are taken from the Amplified® Bible, Copyright © 2015 by The Lockman Foundation. Used by permission.

Scripture quotations marked KJV taken from the King James Version of the Bible.

Scripture quotations marked NIV are taken from The Holy Bible, New International Version®, NIV® Copyright © 1973, 1978, 1984, 2011 by Biblica, Inc.® Used by permission. All rights reserved worldwide.

WestBow Press books may be ordered through booksellers or by contacting:

WestBow Press
A Division of Thomas Nelson & Zondervan
1663 Liberty Drive
Bloomington, IN 47403
www.westbowpress.com
1 (866) 928-1240

Because of the dynamic nature of the Internet, any web addresses or links contained in this book may have changed since publication and may no longer be valid. The views expressed in this work are solely those of the author and do not necessarily reflect the views of the publisher, and the publisher hereby disclaims any responsibility for them.

Any people depicted in stock imagery provided by Getty Images are models, and such images are being used for illustrative purposes only. Certain stock imagery © Getty Images.

ISBN: 978-1-9736-5177-2 (sc)
ISBN: 978-1-9736-5176-5 (hc)
ISBN: 978-1-9736-5178-9 (e)

Library of Congress Control Number: 2019900718

Print information available on the last page.

WestBow Press rev. date: 01/31/2019

CONTENTS

DEDICATION

I dedicate this book to our Lord and Savior, Jesus Christ. I thank you, Lord, for the anointing that rests upon my life. My God, to God be your Glory. It was because of you that I made it through. I thank you for comforting, leading, guiding, healing, delivering, restoring, strengthening, covering, sheltering, and blessing me and for providing for me and my children. I thank you, Lord, for all you have done.

I also dedicate this book to my mother, who has shown me that no matter what we are faced with in life, God is our true answer, and there is no problem too hard for God to solve. I watched you fast, pray, and seek God's face through many trials and tribulations.

You showed me how to seek after and to desire a true relationship with God. You taught me how to forgive those who hurt me.

I saw how God strengthened you and made ways out of no way. I saw how God made things that appeared to be impossible become possible. Through your faith, prayers, and guidance, God provided for us in every area of our lives. I saw God bring you out of a place of bondage and into a place of freedom.

It is because of you that I value and love the Lord the way I do. You have truly taught me as the Word of God says in **Proverbs 22:6, "Train up a child in the way he should go: and when he is old, he will not depart from it" (KJV).** Most of all, I saw God heal your broken heart and set you in a place of peace and stability.

I thank you, Mother, that during my very own process, you took my phone calls any time of the day. You offered much advice from your own experiences. You felt my pain and desired for me to be happy.

You always prayed for me. You always had a godly word to share and prayed for me and my children. So, I thank God for blessing me with such a mighty prayer warrior, Mother; that's who you are. May God, bless you and keep you. I love you, Mother.

Lastly, I would like to dedicate this book to women of all ages who are dealing with the same kinds of issues in their own relationships and marriages. It is my prayer that you seek a relationship with God, who will lead, guide, and direct you into all *truth*. In Jesus name, amen.

ACKNOWLEDGMENTS

I would like to thank everyone who encouraged me to continue moving forward in writing this book. Most importantly, I would like to thank our Lord and Savior, Jesus Christ, whom I love with all my heart. With him, all things are possible, so I honor the Lord for leading me to write this book.

I would also like to thank Dr. Dorothy Jean Smothers—my pastor, spiritual mentor, and counselor. You took my hand and guided me out of a damaged place and helped walk me through this process. I thank you for your prayers, encouragement, phone calls, and texts and for being available whenever I needed you. I am so thankful that the Lord allowed us to cross paths.

I would like to thank God for Mother Renai Fraizier, who has been there for me through thick and thin. I thank God for your prayers, listening ears, telephone calls, texts, concerns, and more. There are no words to explain how grateful I am for you. I thank God for the real love that you've always shown me. May God forever bless you and keep you.

I would also like to thank my children, who continued to encourage me through the ups and downs. I thank my oldest son, who spoke spiritual encouragement into my spirit and gave me the strength I needed to make it through. You always take time out to go with me to different places so that I will not remain in isolation and depression. I am so thankful for you son.

To my only daughter, I thank you for calling me and going on mother/daughter outings to get our manicures and pedicures. You know the girly things I enjoy doing. When you make time for me, it always makes me happy. We have real talks about life, which help me to accept the things that I struggle with. May God, bless you, daughter. I thank God for you.

To my youngest son who fought alongside me to get through these difficult times, I thank you for those private times when we expressed what we both felt about things as a family. We thanked God for giving us strength to move on. Again, son, I say thank you. May God, bless you and keep you.

I would like to thank God for my sister, who listened on the phone to me talk. You made yourself available to listen to my concerns. You sent a word (scripture) through texts to help me throughout my worst days. I thank God for you and appreciate you. May God, bless you and keep you.

I would like to thank God for my friends and extended family members, such as Zarkia Jones, Posha Foreman, and Amanda (close friend) for being there for me when I needed you all. I am forever thankful.

Finally, I thank God for this powerful woman of God who ministered on a "Finish Work". When I would pick, this book up and put it back down, it was this message that pushed me forward. After I heard this message along with another one on Nehemiah; finishing the wall in fifty-two days, I wanted to finish this work. I purposed in my heart to finish this book before the fifty-two days were up. I thank God for his Word, which came forth and inspired me to finish this book. To God be the glory. I bless God for the woman of God I am today.

INTRODUCTION

The purpose of this book is to let women of all ages know there is no situation in which you are stuck. God said in **John 8:36, "So if the Son therefore shall make you free, ye shall be free indeed" (KJV).** With this book, I hope that women will find a relationship with God because he can lead, guide, and direct them in the way they should go regarding their marriages and relationships. Often, decisions are hard to make because of religious beliefs, the time you've invested in a person, the children involved, and most of all, the love that you have for that person.

I share my life experiences to help women who are dealing with problems that may include adultery, infidelity, feeling stuck in a marriage due to religious beliefs, children born during the marriage, and mental, emotional, spiritual, and physical abuse. This book will also highlight how to keep your composure when confronted by the other woman, as well as forgiving all parties involved so that you can be free in your mind, heart, soul, and spirit.

We have all made decisions in our lives that we sometimes regret. Many of us have also sought advice from others by sharing our problems and seeking guidance for the best solutions. There may have also been times when we have shared information with people we shouldn't have. As a result, we have ended up with more hurt than the problem itself caused us. This is because not everyone has your best interests at heart. This was when I decided that God was my true answer.

You will see how God helped me through the process of gaining my life back. He placed the right people in my life at the right time on my path. It was God's strength that gave me a heart to forgive, despite the circumstances.

I had to learn when to speak up and when to hold on to my words when a response was not always necessary. I learned how to hold my peace and let the Lord fight my battles during all the hurt, pain, and betrayal, especially when other women had knowledge that my husband was already married, but they just did not care.

When you turn to God and truly seek him, he will give you your true answer. The Word of the Lord says in **Proverbs 3:5–6, "Trust in the Lord with all my heart and lean not to my own understanding but in all your ways acknowledge him and he will direct your path" (KJV).**

CHAPTER 1

Growing Up

Early Childhood Years

My life as a child was very quiet and full of sadness, optimism, and numbness. I had three siblings and one stepbrother. Their names were Joe (my brother and the second oldest child), Ben (my brother and the third oldest child), Cindy (my sister and the fourth oldest child), and Leon (my stepbrother and the oldest child). I was the youngest of the bunch—the baby girl.

I was born March 25, 1969, in Memphis, Tennessee, at Memphis General Hospital. My mother, Ms. Paulette, was excited to have me, and the delivery went well. After my mother was told we could leave the hospital, she took me to our home, which was a small, flat-topped house in Nashville, Tennessee.

My siblings were excited to have a new baby sister in the house. I remember my mother telling me, when I was around the age of two, that I almost died because I somehow climbed onto the cabinet countertop and swallowed a few of my aunt's birth control pills. My grandmother Tina found me unconscious on the floor of the kitchen. She began to pray for me. She bit me on the lip, and I woke up.

I assume I was taken to the emergency room at the hospital. The medical care team pumped my stomach, stabilized me, and then after some time, released me to go back home. Everyone in my family had been anxious and nervous but had felt better after I had been stabilized. The hospital discharged me to go home with my family in an improved condition.

My mother was an awesome, faithful, hardworking, and true woman of God. My mother did what she had to do to raise us. I remember her working two jobs solely to make sure we had a roof over our heads and food on the table for every meal. She made it her mission to involve us heavily in the church and to understand the ways of the Lord.

Unfortunately, she married someone who did not follow the ways of the Lord. This person was our stepfather, and he had a son. After a while, his son also came to live with us too.

Because our stepfather did not believe and follow the Lord, our family faced many different challenges, obstacles, frustrations, emotional pains, and heartaches. We were forced to move approximately fourteen times due to his lack of contributions and accountability to our family. Because of my stepfather, we encountered much instability beginning in early childhood years all the way up through my adolescents.

When I was three or four, my mother decided to relocate to Daytona Beach, Florida. From what I have been told, I know that my biological father was consistently involved in my life from the time I was born. This move caused great problems for my biological father since he was no longer able to see me frequently.

I ended up having to move to Vero Beach, Florida, with my grandmother. She took me to church every Sunday and taught me about God. She always said to me, "Baby, don't ever play with the Lord. Always take God seriously." I resided with my grandmother only a couple of years. While I was living with her, my father could see me more often again.

When I was around four years old, my father picked me up from my grandmother's home to spend some time with me. We went to a takeout restaurant that he owned. Because I was so young at the time, I only remember the time we went there and an altercation took place, which ultimately took my father's life. I do not remember what specifically happened, but I do remember my father being rushed to the emergency room and me being taken to a nearby relative's home. Shortly afterward, I learned that my father had died on the way to the hospital. At that age, I did not understand that I would never be able to see my father again. When I would lie down in bed at night with my grandmother, she was always there to comfort, pray with, and talk to me about the ways of the Lord.

I remained with my grandmother only a couple more months. Then my Aunt Peach took me to Daytona Beach to live with my mother, siblings, and stepfather. The tension in the house was evident at the time. My stepfather had been unfaithful and abusive verbally, emotionally, and physically. He lacked the responsibility to take care of our home's financial affairs.

At the time, he was a construction worker. Therefore, his employment assignments varied from part-time to full-time jobs. During certain seasons, there was no work for him at all. He also went out and had affairs with various women. He would claim that he had paid the mortgage, but my mother would find out that the payments had never been made. She had to carry the burden paying for the mortgage and all the other bills, so she was forced to get a second job.

Unfortunately, even with the second job, my mother still was unable to maintain our household, which led her to seek financial help from someone at the church we were attending. Even though my mother was doing so much for our family, our stepfather continued to lie about paying the mortgage. Our family was extremely unstable, which caused us to have to move constantly.

Any time my mother was away at work, my stepfather would come home and look for things to argue with her about once she got home. When my mother finally confronted him about his affairs and financial obligations to the family, he became verbally and physically abusive to her. Due to his own personal issues, he also took out his frustrations on the boys of the family. He used outrageous disciplinary measures on a regular basis, such as hitting them with a water hose or an extension cord.

Around this time, I remember going to a babysitter's house since I was too young to go to school. Feeling overwhelmed by the issues at home, I did not want to be around the other children. So, one day after I was dropped off, I left the premises and tried to make my way back home. I was walking through the neighborhood and crying since I didn't know how to get back to my home or the babysitter's house.

Someone from the neighborhood stopped and asked me, "What is wrong?"

I replied, "I don't know how to get back to the lady who keeps me. I walked away."

The police were called. They took me back to the lady at the day care, who called my mother. The day care teacher was in a panic and did not understand why I had walked away. I didn't know how to express my feelings to her because I was a child. My mother did not know that watching all the abuse I had to endure made me afraid that my stepfather was going to seriously hurt her or one of my siblings.

Although the babysitter loved my mother, after that incident, she was afraid to keep me again. This left my mother in an unfortunate situation of trying to find someone else to watch me. Eventually, she was able to find a church member to do this.

Due to the previously mentioned financial issues, we remained in the same financial problems. My mother did not feel comfortable going back to the same church member for help again since my mother still owed her for the first loan she had borrowed. My mother couldn't afford to pay the mortgage as well as the other bills. My stepfather continued to have affairs and used his money outside of our home. Eventually, our home went into foreclosure, and we were forced to leave the premises immediately. After this, my mother, siblings, and I moved back to Tampa, Florida, to live with my grandmother. My stepfather stayed in Daytona Beach to reside with the women he had been sleeping with.

My mother's former employer at a nursing facility in Daytona Beach hired her back. I was finally old enough to enter school and attended Great Levine Elementary School in Vero Beach, Florida. While we were living with my grandmother, she helped us out tremendously. She even assisted my mother in getting a car.

A few months after we settled in Vero Beach, my stepfather called and asked my mother to come and get him from Daytona Beach. My mother and my stepfather's brother went to pick him up, and on the way back, the car broke down. Another family member went to pick them up, and they continued to south Florida. The next day, my stepfather and his brother returned to get the car so that they could fix it. We stayed with my grandmother, and my stepfather went to live with his own family.

My mother continued to work and eventually saved up enough money to rent another home. Once she did this, we moved out of my grandmother's home and into our own place. My stepfather eventually joined us there. The new area we lived in was called Mountain Blake Apartments. I had to change schools to Northview Elementary since it was closer to our new home.

Not long after we settled into the new place, the chaos with my stepfather started up again. He consistently cheated, lied, partially worked, and began to physically assault my mother again. I was always quiet and unhappy but observant. At a young age, I remember going to school most days feeling depressed and sad about the reality I was forced to deal with at home. Less than a year after we had settled into the new place, we were forced to move again due to the apartment community closing.

My mother found another house to rent in an area called Blue Hill Terrace, but I still attended Northview Elementary School during my second- and third-grade years. Although, we had moved out of the district of that school, my mother did not want us to change schools again, so she drove us to school every day.

My mother started praying every morning with my siblings and me before we went to school. We also began attending a local church every Sunday and eventually became active members. We attended church on Tuesday and Thursday nights and youth choir rehearsal on Friday nights.

While we were living in this home, my stepfather started having another affair with a woman who lived across the street as well as with another woman that lived nearby. At times, we couldn't even attend church services because my stepfather would take a mechanical part out of her car with him, just to spite my mother. Once he took the car keys and threw them onto the roof of the house in the rain to keep us from going to church.

He continued to physically and verbally assault my mother whenever she confronted him about his various affairs. On one occasion, my mother's friend who lived down the street called her at work and told her to come home. She said, "If you come home now, you will catch him at the other woman's house."

When my mom came home, she went over to the house where my stepfather was and caught him there. He claimed there was nothing going on, but the affair continued after this incident. When he came back to our house, he was very violent and physically fought my mother. Some days, she would have swollen, black-and-blue eyes and a very defeated, sad look on her face. This made me so emotional that I cried and had the worst stomach pains.

My siblings and I started to develop strong feelings of hatred toward him. We began to talk amongst ourselves and say, "Why won't she just leave him?" His biological son wanted to physically hurt him.

Even with everything he put my mother through, she always taught us that we were not supposed to hate anyone. She said, "It is wrong to hate people. You should hate the act of sin and not the person."

My siblings would ask, "Why do you stay in this marriage?"

My mother explained that she had been taught that she was

not supposed to leave her marriage. As a result, she stayed in the marriage, and my siblings and I continued to suffer in an unhealthy environment, unhappiness, and frustration.

The affair my stepfather was having with the neighbor from across the street eventually ended. However, he started another affair with a woman who lived near his mother. He rarely went to work. While my mother was at work, he spent most of his time with other women.

My mother was still handling all the finances, such as paying all the utility bills, buying groceries, buying school clothes and supplies, and paying insurance. My stepfather was supposed to be the one paying for our rent. My stepfather stole this money from our family. He lied and said he was paying the rent. We quickly found out that he hadn't been because we were forced to move again.

At this point, my mother and siblings went back to reside with my grandmother for the summer. I went to my Aunt Samantha's house in Vero Beach, Florida. My stepfather went back to live with his family.

While visiting my Aunt Samantha during the summer, she would perm and take care of my hair. One day, she and I were talking about my biological father. My aunt revealed to me that he had been married to another woman when I had been conceived. My heart was broken by the news, as I did not know this information. My aunt apologized to me. She had assumed I had already known this.

When I saw my mother, I asked her about what my aunt had revealed to me. She decided to sit me down and to explain. She had found out that my father was married when she was eight months pregnant with me. She mentioned that a friend had told her about his marriage and had informed my mother who his wife was. When she had confronted my father about this, he had said that he had not got around to telling her.

Because my mother's friend had pointed out who my father's wife was, one day, my mother stopped the lady and told her that she was sorry and that she had not known he had been married. His wife replied, "If it had not been you, it would have been someone else."

My mother explained to me that because her pregnancy had been from a married man, she had not wanted to raise me. Then she had decided to give me to my Aunt Samantha (whom I had stayed with for the summer).

As soon as I was born, she had changed her mind and had decided she was not going to give me up. After my mother shared this information with me, I began to feel rejected and unloved by my own mother. She also told me who my other siblings were on my father's side. They knew who I was, but I did not know them. I learned that they lived one street over from my Aunt Samantha's house. Since I was very young, I did not want to go over and meet them. I wasn't sure how they would feel about me because I was a child conceived outside of a marriage.

Just before summer was over, my mother found another home in Greenville Acres, Florida, so my family relocated there. However, I stayed with my Aunt Samantha until summer break ended. After that, I went to reside with my mother, siblings, and stepfather. My sister and I shared a room, and my brothers shared a room. We were happy to have our own space again. My mother registered my siblings and me at the local schools. By this time, I was in fourth grade and attended Greenville Oaks Elementary School up until the fifth grade.

While residing in this area, we fell back into the same cycle of problems: My stepfather's affairs continued, he lied about paying the rent, and it all led up to us being evicted once again. One day, all our belongings and everything we loved were placed outside on the grass. This totally embarrassed my siblings and me. The other children in the neighborhood talked about us. That day, my oldest brother had to stay at the house instead of going to school so people wouldn't steal our things.

When my mother came home from work, we had to immediately find another place to live. We ended up moving into my stepfather's aunt's (Sally) garage. Instead of looking for somewhere else to stay, my stepfather was out fooling around with different women. He refused to work. When he did work, he did not bring the money home to help pay bills. We remained in this location for about two months.

One day, my oldest brother, Joe, was playing with Aunt Sally's dog. The dog bit him. The dog's bite had just missed a main artery near my brother's neck, and he was rushed to the hospital where he had to get stitches. After this incident, Aunt Sally was so afraid for our safety, she told us that we had to move. At this point, we moved in with a cousin in Little City, Florida.

After a couple of weeks, we moved again from there to Greenville Acres because my mother's friend allowed her to take over her apartment. Somehow, the owner of the apartments found out and told my mother we could not do that because there was a list of people waiting for the apartments, so we were forced to move again. My mother, sister, stepfather, and I ended up staying in a one-room motel while my brothers resided with my grandmother in Vero Beach, Florida.

The motel was disgusting and not at all up to clean-living standards. We had to share a bathroom with everyone in the motel. I was so embarrassed about our situation I did not even want to tell my friends where I lived. My sister and I would watch out for each other as we showered since there were so many strange people who lurked in the bathroom area.

We stayed there for a month until we found a one-bedroom apartment in Little City. Then we moved there to bring everyone together again. All the siblings slept in the living room, and my mother and stepfather stayed in the bedroom. However, my stepfather was hardly there because he was with his other women.

Soon after moving in, the owner of the apartments told us we had to move out because there were too many of us to live in the one-bedroom apartment. So, we found a two-bedroom house to rent in another part of Little City.

CHAPTER 2

My Middle School Years

A t this time of my life, I started middle school. My other siblings were old enough to get jobs, so they worked at various fast-food restaurants. My sister played basketball for the local school. I got into cheerleading and playing softball to keep busy and away from all the chaos at our home.

In the meantime, I found out that my cousin, who was working at our local grocery store, knew my siblings on my father's side. I still had not seen or met them because I had moved to Daytona Beach with my mother soon after my father had passed away. I had only been about eight years old when my aunt Samantha had told me the truth about my father, so I had no clue who my siblings were or what they looked like.

Nevertheless, my cousin saw one of my brothers one day while she was at work and told him of my whereabouts. I still remember the day he came over to my house and introduced himself to me. I was so happy to finally meet him. He informed me that my other siblings were excited to meet me as well.

When I eventually did meet all my siblings, I could tell they lived in nice homes and were happy with their lives. Knowing how much of a wreck my own home was, I remained quiet and always pretended to be happy around them.

As time went by, they began coming to see me on a regular

basis and supporting me at my softball games. My sisters would also come and invite me to different family functions too. I felt like this was finally a positive factor in my life, which had been filled with so much negativity.

At my own home, however, I continued to deal with the arguments, affairs, and chaos. One day, I got so fed up with the negativity I was living in, I decided that I had enough. I made the decision to end my life, not knowing the true consequences of this decision. I took a knife and was about to stab myself in the stomach when someone came home, so I did not go through with it.

Because of this failed attempt, I began having stomach problems and would get sick every time I learned that my mother had an altercation with my stepfather. Eventually I found the time to talk to my mother alone about how I felt. She expressed that she understood.

She began trying to keep things from me, but I always knew when something was going on. I went back to my aunt's house on the weekends to get away from my living nightmare. While there, I was able to find peace and felt as if I had a family because my uncle and aunt treated me as if I was their own child.

Due to all the fighting at my home, the police were called several times. They would come, talk to my stepfather, and advise him to leave. He would always leave but then would end up coming right back.

One day, my second to oldest brother, Ben, got so upset because of the fighting, cheating, and chaos that went on with my stepfather, he went and got a gun to shoot him. He waited up through the night for my stepfather to walk through the door. However, that night, my stepfather did not come home. We thank God for this because this plan could have ended in my brother being sent to jail or in something he would have to deal with for the rest of his life.

On another occasion, my mother and stepfather were fighting because she had confronted him about his affairs. In the middle of the argument, she got on her knees and started praying. While she was there, he tried to strike her in the face. As his arm swung down, his wrist split open and blood went everywhere. He kept saying, "What do you have on you?"

She just kept praying the scripture found in **Mark 9:42, that says, "And whosoever shall offend one of these little ones that believe in me, it is better for him that a millstone were hanged about his neck, and he were cast into the sea" (KJV).**

He then grabbed a towel, wrapped it tightly around his arm, and rushed to the emergency room. After this incident, he never hit her again. However, due to so many domestic violence incidents and police callings, the owner of this house told us we had to move. My sister, my mother, and I moved in with a cousin, and my brothers had to move back in with my grandmother. My stepfather went back to his family and of course, continued his lifestyle of affairs.

By this time, I was in seventh grade and would soon be moving up to eighth. My sister was in high school. She still played basketball for her school. I continued to cheerlead and play softball. I finally began to have fun and enjoyed being around friends. In the meantime, my mother continued to look for another place, as we needed to move out of my cousin's house and into our own space.

My mother started looking for another place, but for the first time, it was without my stepfather. After much prayer and patience, she found a house in Honey Oak, Florida, on her own. This was where I resided until I left home. Finally, we were all excited to have our own place of stability and happiness without the presence of our stepfather.

He did make several attempts to try to come to that location, but every attempt was denied. Around that time, I was in the eighth grade and ready to move on to high school.

I can honestly say that at this point, I began to experience stability and happiness. My mother was able to buy my sister a car, and we drove to school together every day so we could continue attending the same schools we had been attending. Eventually, my sister went off to college, and I continued driving to high school throughout my four years there.

CHAPTER 3

My High School Years

During my high school years, I played basketball and worked during the summers to keep myself busy and to reach my future goals and plans. I was determined to stay focused and make it to college.

In my sophomore year, I met the craziest girl who became my best friend over time. Her name was Amanda. She also talked me into joining the high school band. I had no idea how to play any instruments, but this band played the type of music that I liked. I loved to dance. So, one day, I followed her advice, came to practice, and just jumped in line.

When the band director saw me, he said, "Where did you come from?"

I said, "She told me to come and get in line."

The band director was very cool. He did not say much. He just laughed and shook his head.

In the meantime, I had to learn how to play an instrument. So, I took band classes and learned how to play the cymbals and just a little bit of percussion. I only wanted to be in the band, so it didn't matter what instrument they needed me to play.

We traveled on several different occasions and had so much fun in the band. I was truly happy during my high school years.

By the time, I was in the tenth grade and just about to go into the eleventh, my mother bought me a car. She gave me strict rules concerning the car, and I obeyed every single one of them. I was allowed to pick up my best friend every day, and we drove to school together.

My best friend and I went many places together, dressed alike, shared many ups and downs, and supported each other. Yet at some point down the line, we both made wrong decisions.

CHAPTER 4

Making a Wrong Decision

My best friend and I agreed that we would not take dating seriously until we got well into our college years. In our junior and senior years of high school, my best friend met a guy named Bruce and began dating him. She did not inform me that she was seeing this young man until sometime later that year. My friend continued to date him throughout our senior year.

I had a vehicle, so she would ask me to drive her to his apartment sometimes. I would drop her off, or he would pick her up from her apartment where she resided with her aunt and cousins. Then I would either go home or sit with her at her place for a little while.

On one occasion, my friend and I were at a Popeyes in my area. As we were ordering our food, a young man came into the Popeyes and began staring at me. After we purchased our order, I noticed that the young man was still watching me. I smiled a little from the attention he was showing me.

As my friend and I were walking out to our car, he came out right behind us. His car was parked next to us, so I looked over at him and smiled. He smiled back and asked me what my name was. The conversation between us flowed so freely, and we exchanged phone numbers.

Through my communication with him, I found out that he played football at one of our rival high schools, but we continued to get acquainted with one another. We both talked about our plans for college. I explained to him that I was not taking any relationships seriously, at that time, because I wanted to stay focused on college.

Eventually, we started meeting up with each other. He would come by my home, or I would go to his house with my best friend. I never went alone, as I was always too scared to do so.

We continued to see each other for a couple more months, and sure enough, he began to ask intimate questions. I explained to him multiple times that I did not want to be intimate with anyone because I wanted to stay focused on college.

He was a handsome, nicely built young man who played sports very well. I felt that once he got to college there would be other females wanting to hook up with him, so I never took him that seriously. I was also trying to see if he was only after one thing, so I always paid close attention to his actions. Nevertheless, we continued talking on the phone with occasional visits.

He then began saying things like, "If you take care of me, I will take care of you." This was a big turnoff for me, so I decreased my contact with him. This also made me feel that he was only after one thing, which went totally against what I believed. I had not been sexually involved with anyone. I was a virgin. I wanted to save myself for my husband.

As I began to pull back from this young man, I would go to different places where the young people would go on the weekends. One weekend, I went to the movies. While in the movie, I looked down a couple of rows and saw the young man sitting with his friends and another young lady, who was right beside him. I was not angry, but it did prove to me what I had thought from the beginning.

When I confronted him about the situation, he claimed that the young lady was a friend of his friend. I did not believe this, so I continued to decrease my association with him. We went from seeing each other to just talking on the phone. I told him that I did not want that kind of relationship and did not want to take anyone seriously. We decided to see other people and only maintain a friendship. We also said if it was meant to be then we would meet back up again after we had pursued our goals.

In the meantime, my best friend continued dating her guy friend. I was determined to remain single and not to date despite her decision.

We took the necessary steps to submit our applications for college and to take college entrance exams. I desired to attend Florida Beach University because I wanted to be in its marching band. I had remained in band during high school.

I got accepted at Florida Beach University but had to attend summer classes. However, my friend was unable to attend for personal reasons. She then applied to State Mountain College in New York and was accepted there. I had always wanted to go to New York, so I also applied at this school and was accepted. We decided that we would attend college together.

As the end of our high school year approached, we prepared for prom night. I attended prom at our school with an all-American football player. My friend attended the prom with her boyfriend.

After prom, my date wanted to attend the after party. I told him I wanted to go home. I was home by midnight. I had been taught to come in at a respectful hour and to behave myself like a young lady. Many things happened on prom night, but I came home.

During the summer, my friend and I prepared to leave for college. When we got to the college, my paperwork and my room and board were already in order. Because my friend had become so involved with her boyfriend, she had been unable to get her paperwork completed. She ended up having to leave the campus. This left me alone and in a very difficult situation.

When she had left home, my friend had told me that her family members had said she could not come back. As a result, my friend had nowhere to go. I felt sorry for her, so I took the initiative to drive her back home to Florida where she ended up living with her boyfriend. At this point, I was offered a partial scholarship to play in the marching band at Kentucky Hill University the following semester, which would be the beginning of January.

While I was waiting to leave for college for the second time, I learned through my friend that her boyfriend had an older brother who wanted to meet me. Right away, I responded that I did not want to get involved with anyone because I was going to college. Nevertheless, my best friend kept her relationship going, and her boyfriend ended up in jail.

I had to take her to his older brother's house to receive his collect phone calls from jail. During this time, the older brother casually spoke to me. It was never anything serious. I was not interested in talking to him because he hustled for money in the streets and was well known for this by a lot of people. He had a male roommate that he was sharing an apartment with.

Just about every week, I would take my friend to their house so that she could receive the phone call from her boyfriend. While she was waiting for his call, we would all talk, laugh, and have fun. One day when we came over, I noticed there was a little boy, who looked like he was around the age of nine. I assumed this was the roommate's child.

As time went on, the older brother began to talk a little more seriously to me. He asked me if I would consider having a relationship with him. I said that I wouldn't because I would be going off to college. He said he wouldn't mind waiting for me. I kind of laughed it off because I did not take him seriously. He was totally different from what I wanted in a boyfriend. He was on the streets hustling people for a living. I told him I did not want anybody that was hustling on a corner. I told him that I attended church and believed in doing things the right way.

As we continued to meet, our conversations got more and more intense. He continued to pursue a relationship with me. We would often sit and have long conversations about it. We eventually exchanged phone numbers and continued to talk via the telephone on the days I did not go over to his house with my friend. Eventually,

I set boundaries. I told him what I did not want in a man and the things that he had to do to be considered relationship material for me. We also discussed my plans for going away to college. At that time, I was about nineteen years old.

In November 1988, I decided to give the relationship a try. In other words, I made the wrong decision!

CHAPTER 5

My Experiences in the Relationship

I Settled Despite What I Knew

We began dating and seeing each other on a regular basis. We shared many different things with each other about ourselves. My boyfriend cleaned up his surroundings and stopped so many different people from coming in and out of his apartment. He stopped hustling in the streets and got a decent job. He changed his phone number and forced people to respect our relationship.

I was surprised that he was willing to change those things so that he could have a relationship with me. We also talked about what we needed to do to maintain the relationship when outsiders tried to interfere. I felt we were honest about everything, no matter what we encountered. I felt we had a very good relationship in the beginning.

Because I had always been a church girl, I respected the things that I had been taught growing up. Either I left his house at a decent hour or he came to my house. My mother always said, "A woman should not run behind a man, but the man should come see the woman."

When my family found out whom I was dating, they were not pleased with my choice due to his prior lifestyle. They were not aware of the changes he had made to be in a relationship with me. My boyfriend also began attending the church where I was a devoted member.

As we continued this relationship, we grew closer and closer. We began to go places and do things together as a couple. We spent a lot of time together. He shared many things that had happened in his childhood. I shared things I had experienced while growing up. There was not a day that went by when we did not see each other. I would go to his house after work, or he would come to my house after he got off from work. When we did not see each other in person, we would fall asleep while we were talking on the phone to each other. He would always tell me that he wanted what was his to be all his, and I would tell him that I wanted what was mine to be all mine. Additionally, he mentioned that he was a very jealous person. We both said that we loved each other.

One night, things went a little further. I lost my virginity to my boyfriend. Afterward, I felt very uncomfortable. So many things went through my mind. I kept telling myself that this was not what was supposed to happen. How could I have let this happen?

I sinned. I repented. Nevertheless, we continued dating. Now that we were intimate, we were emotionally and spiritually connected.

On Sunday afternoons, I would go to the football field to watch my boyfriend play flag football just for fun with other friends. One of those days, I noticed that the same little boy I had seen the first time was at the house again. He went with us to the park, so I asked my boyfriend, "Whose little boy is this?"

My boyfriend said, "I thought you knew he was my son."

Immediately, I got very quiet. Then I said, "You never told me you had a son. I thought he was your roommate's son."

I was very hurt and did not want a ready-made family. I was not ready to be a mother to someone as I was going to college. I felt he should have told me about the boy at the beginning, but he hadn't. I was disappointed in him. I felt he should have told me to see if I was willing to accept that responsibility. However, love was such a powerful thing, and since I loved him, I continued the relationship.

Soon enough, it was time for me to go off to college at Kentucky Hill University. We made promises to each other to keep the relationship going. He promised to come and see me, and I promised to come home and be with him.

As the school year began, it was difficult to be so far away from family. I got homesick and eventually went back home with a new goal of attending a local community college. I felt like such a failure. I desired to complete college and earn my degree but had yet to accomplish it.

When I was home, of course I ended up right back with my boyfriend while I went to a business school and earned a certification in business technology. I also got a part-time job at a department store while attending school. My boyfriend continued working at his job. When we got together after work, we enjoyed lounging around, watching television, and spending time with each other. Our relationship went very well throughout the remainder of that year until Christmas of December 1990.

On Christmas day, my boyfriend, my friend, and I went to his mother's house to meet his family. My boyfriend surprised me and bought me a promise ring. I was very happy about the ring. My friend and I were laughing and celebrating the ring. We had a wonderful time that day until I went in the house to meet his family.

As I was sitting there, I noticed quite a few children running around and playing. I asked my friend, "Who are all these children?"

She began to point them out and say who the parents were. However, when she got to one little girl who was about five and a little boy who was about six, she said, "Those are your boyfriend's kids."

I said, "What?"

She said, "Yes. I thought you knew he had kids."

I said, "No."

Immediately, I was upset. I went outside and asked my boyfriend, "Why didn't you tell me you had kids?" I was in tears. I snatched the promise ring off and threw it as far away from me as possible. I was so mad. I said, "This is not fair." I cried, left, and went back to my home in Honey Oaks.

My boyfriend kept calling me and saying he was sorry. I said, "This is not fair. You did not tell me. Why didn't you tell me about the other two kids when you told me about your first little boy?" I kept weeping, and he kept apologizing. I told him that I never wanted to speak to him again.

The next day, I heard a knock at the front door. I went and answered it, knowing it was my boyfriend. As soon as the door opened, he immediately began expressing how sorry he was for not telling me. He also said he thought that I had known that they were his kids.

"You were supposed to tell me, whether I knew or not," I said to him. "I am not ready to be someone else's mother."

He told me that he loved me and that he did not want the relationship to end. Despite the circumstances, I loved him too and did not want the relationship to end either, so I told him to give me some time to think everything over. Even though I told him to be patient, he continued to come around and called often to check on me.

We missed spending time together since we were used to seeing each other every day, so we eventually started seeing each other again. Although, I was still hurt about the situation, my emotions were involved, and it became difficult for me to walk away. I found myself settling and accepting the situation even though this was not what I wanted. Again, I let down my standards and continued to date him.

Sometimes his kids were around and sometimes they weren't. When they were around, I would try to bond with them but did not know how to since I was not trying to be a mother at that time. I felt extremely turned off by my boyfriend but still loved him and wanted to make it work. All of this was very hard for me to process. I did enjoy the time he and I spent together when the kids were not around. I believe that because of those few happy times, I remained in the relationship.

Our picture-perfect relationship was shaken as soon as the

baby momma drama came knocking. When the mother of the two children found out we were dating, she began to try to break up our relationship.

One night, we were together at his apartment, and she decided to come over unannounced. My boyfriend went outside and asked her to leave multiple times. She became angry and tried to run him over with her car and then hit my car on purpose. I had a very nice two-door red Toyota Supra. My boyfriend was so angry he called the police on her. He also followed the mother of his children back to her place and ended up in a fight with a young man that she was seeing at the time.

In the meantime, I was at the apartment waiting for the police. When the police finally came, I filed charges against her. This was just the beginning of a long journey full of highs and lows.

Once my boyfriend returned to his apartment, he found me anxiously waiting for him. He looked at me, pulling me in for a hug, and said, "I am sorry. I will get your car fixed." He did get my car repaired, but we kept the bill so that we could submit the total charges to be repaid by the mother of his children. A court hearing was eventually scheduled, but she did not appear. Therefore, a bench warrant was issued for her arrest.

Although, I was highly frustrated with my relationship, I continued seeing my boyfriend because I loved him. Everything had been going so well for us, but soon enough, situations with his children's mother had begun to resurface. She continued to create problems within our relationship.

I started feeling very hurt and confused and thought the relationship was not going to work. My boyfriend and I had moments where we would sit and talk about our difficulties. Regardless of how we were both hurt by this situation, we still tried to maintain a good relationship and to be happy together because we still loved each other.

We continued dating and spending time with each other daily for about two more years. We went to clubs together and just had a lot of fun. I had always been a church girl, so I did not know a lot about clubs and did not drink at all. On the other hand, my boyfriend was a heavy drinker.

I hadn't been aware that he drank as much as he did, so this created new issues for us. I expressed my concern to him, and he respected me enough not to drink around me. Because he had a history of dating different women before he knew me, new problems arose from those other. Some women were extremely jealous of our relationship and tried different tactics to cause problems for us, but my boyfriend would always set the situation straight. He maintained respect for our relationship at that time.

Eventually, he started going to the clubs with his friends who were single, and we experienced more serious problems. My boyfriend started drinking heavily. There were times that he could come home from the club with his friends very drunk. I would always make sure he was okay. Then I would go home and wait until the next day when I knew he was sober so that I could talk to him.

Sure enough, the next day, I went to his apartment to talk to him. I expressed my concern with him getting so drunk. I was trying to see if this was a pattern or something he was doing because he had a problem. Nevertheless, he promised that he would try to stop drinking so much. Again, I settled and decided to stay in the relationship because I loved him.

Our relationship went on as usual. We continued to spend time together. I noticed that the time we spent together began to dwindle. On the weekends, he went from spending his time with me to spending his time in the clubs with friends drinking again. I couldn't understand why things began to go downhill. I figured the club scene must've really been something special since he wanted to be there so often, so I went out to the clubs where I knew he would be. Although, I did not like this kind of club, as I was not a club person, I just wanted to get out and go there because I knew he would be there.

One Saturday, I decided to go to a little club that people called

A Place to Be club. There was one way in and one way out. It was a very small space. However, it was a place where a lot of the young to middle-aged adults would hang out. When my boyfriend noticed, I was there, he got a little upset.

I wondered, *Why is it that he can go to the club but does not want me to come here?* My boyfriend explained that he was a very jealous person and did not want anybody trying to come on to me at that club.

I then said, "If that is the case, then you should not be here either." I also said to him, "I am not staying home every weekend while you go out with your friends."

Again, I went back to the apartment and waited for him. Sure enough, he came home sloppy drunk once again. At this point, I felt a little frustrated and did not understand what was going on. I had told him many times how I felt about him going out so much and about his heavy drinking, but it seemed as if it didn't matter to him.

I waited for him to sober up so that we could talk again. I explained my concern about his getting drunk. He apologized again and said he was going to quit drinking. For a while, he did not go out at all, and when he did go out, we went together. We went back to spending a lot of time together. He started telling his friends he was going to stay home with his girlfriend.

We began to talk things over and agreed to take our relationship one day at a time. I felt as if our relationship was going back to where it had started. In my mind, we were both happier than we had ever been. Our focus was always on each other and making sure we were always there for one another.

I remember that on one occasion, we went to the local fair. He played a basketball game and won me a teddy bear. However, it was not the teddy bear that the man had promised my boyfriend would win. The man gave him a little teddy bear, so my boyfriend got upset and whispered to me, "I have money in a certain place. Bond me out of jail."

I immediately said, "It is not worth it. Please do not hit this man." After my boyfriend confronted the man, the man gave him the big teddy bear. I was very nervous and embarrassed after this. I just wanted to leave. Because I had been raised in the church, I was not used to that kind of behavior.

My boyfriend apologized to me. We left and went back to his apartment to talk things over. He was very concerned with the way I felt about things, so we focused on how we could make things right.

Despite all the signs that pointed I should walk out of the relationship, I chose to stay in it because I loved him. I hoped so hard and so much that our relationship would work, no matter what we went through. Again, I was settling and accepting things I wasn't comfortable with. His old habits quickly returned, and the cycles of his terrible tendencies were present again. He would go out and come back drunk. Then we would talk, I would forgive him, and we would make up.

Our relationship continued for about two more years with him drinking and going out to clubs. I noticed that his drinking really got out of hand as he began mixing drinks like E and J and coke, gin, and juice. He drank heavily to the point where his friends had to bring him home to make sure he was okay. He would stumble into the apartment and vomit everywhere. I was so upset, I would leave him in the middle of the floor. Many nights, I remember crying and wondering what made him feel like he needed to drink so much.

Although I had not totally given my life to God, I was not a bad person. I didn't feel that I deserved to be going through this. I still went to church faithfully every Sunday. With this being said, I had a dream that a girl was saying she was pregnant by my boyfriend. After the dream, I woke up praying that it wasn't true. When I told my boyfriend about the dream, he reassured me that it was just a dream and that it would never happen.

Well one day, I visited my cousin's house. As I was talking to my cousin, her boyfriend, Bobbie, asked if I knew a certain person.

I said, "I know of this person."

He said, "I ran into her one day and saw that she was pregnant.

I asked, 'Who are you pregnant from?' and she gave me your boyfriend's name."

I was very hurt but did not show it to my cousin's boyfriend. I left, went straight to my boyfriend, and told him what had happened. Immediately, he denied knowing anything about her pregnancy or having any relations with her. The fact that another woman was even saying she was carrying his child was heartbreaking. Again, he grabbed me and reassured me that this was not his child.

I knew the woman's number because my boyfriend was friends with her brother. One day, I called her and asked if she was pregnant from my boyfriend. She asked who had told me this. I then explained to her that my cousin's boyfriend had told me.

She then said to me, "I saw Bobbie, and he asked me who was I pregnant from. I told him, and he said that the guy had a girlfriend. I then said that I knew it and didn't care."

Although I was very hurt, I said to her, "Well, he is saying that it is not his child."

She said, "Believe him then."

I then started to laugh at her until she said, 'Please don't laugh at me.'"

After the phone call, I went back to my boyfriend and confronted him again. He continued to deny that the child was his and that he had had any previous relations with her.

I said to him, "Nobody is going to say they are pregnant from you if you did not sleep with them."

After many hours of interrogation, he finally admitted to cheating with this individual. However, he continued to deny that the child was his.

I was very heartbroken. I kept asking myself how a person could love someone and have relations with someone else. I pondered this every day. I told myself that I would never hurt anybody or sleep with someone else's boyfriend. How could someone do this to me and not care?

My boyfriend stayed right there with me as I hurt and cried. He held me, crying, apologizing, and begging me for my forgiveness.

I kept asking him, "How could you do this?" At that point, I told him that this was not going to work and moved out of the house we shared and went back home.

Of course, he did not leave me alone. I tried to get through the process of the hurting alone, but it was hard. He kept coming to my house, saying he was sorry, and asking for my forgiveness. I said, "I cannot anymore. This is too much."

Being he would not stop pursuing me, he asked me to go to a local fair. I decided to go with him because I still loved him. I just wanted to get out of the house and away from the temporary hurt I was going through.

That night, we got on one of the rides that flipped us upside down and went all around. I got very nauseous on this ride and began to vomit. After we got off the ride, I continued throwing up. We went back to the car, and I threw up on the way to the car. As we rode in the car, he had to pull over so I could throw up again. Finally, we went to McDonald's and got some ice cream. I ate the ice cream, and the vomiting ceased.

As time went by, I missed my cycle, so I went to the doctor's office to see what was going on. I found out that I was pregnant. I went back home and broke down crying again. When I called my boyfriend, and told him I was pregnant, he got so excited and happy. I told him I was honestly considering an abortion. He begged me not to do so.

After going back and forth in my mind and knowing that abortion was wrong, I decided to keep the child. I carried the child with much grief, anger, frustration, and the thought that there might also be another woman who was carrying his child. In the meantime, the rumors concerning the other woman never ceased.

As time went on, my stomach began to grow, and others learned that I was pregnant. This was a very embarrassing and emotional time for me.

Because my boyfriend was afraid that I would leave him, he continued to drink heavily. He liked to play pool, so every now and then, he would go to a local billiards club to play pool with the other guys. Whenever he came back to the apartment, I could see that he was weighed down with many problems and that he was continuing to drink.

By this time, I did not have much to say, as I was very hurt and confused. Again, the same pattern continued. He would say, "I am sorry. Please forgive me." In addition to this, he still denied that the other woman's child was his. Because I carried his child and was so in love with him, I continued to stay in the relationship feeling hurt and confused.

One day, my boyfriend went up to the corner store. While he was there, the police came up there and began to question him. According to him, he had been sitting on a motorcycle that had no license plate or tag, so they had harassed him. My boyfriend had the rent money on him, so they had taken it out of his pockets. He said that when they had put the money back, it had not been the original amount he had on him. When he questioned them about this, things began to get aggressive, which led to his arrest.

When his court date came, he was sentenced to three years in prison. He was required to do a year and a half with a reduced sentence due to good behavior. I was left all alone, being two-months pregnant and soon to have my first child. Again, I felt hurt, alone, and disappointed. During the time he was incarcerated, I accepted his phone calls and visited him while still trying to process the hurt along with everything else. I often said to myself. *This is not how I wanted my first relationship to be*—or any relationship for that matter.

I continued in this place of sadness, aloneness, and depression while pregnant. The rumors about the other individual's pregnancy never stopped. I soon learned that she was having her baby four months prior to my due date. I still did not know the truth as he still denied that the child was his.

After the other woman's pregnancy, I had not seen the child and neither had my boyfriend because of his incarceration. I decided to put this aside and to focus on my own health as well as my own child.

Four months later, I had my baby. I was happy for my child but sad that I had given birth to this child without his father. My mother stayed by my side throughout this process, as I was very scared. Now I had to learn how to be a good mother while trying to stay encouraged despite my circumstances.

On the other hand, my boyfriend was happy to learn of his new baby boy's birth and proceeded to tell me what to name him. Although incarcerated, the father of my child seemed very much concerned for our well-being.

After two days, I was released from the hospital. I went home and began to take care of my newborn baby. After about six weeks, I took him to the correctional facility to see his father for the first time. His father was very happy to see him. I was also happy to see how he bonded with his newborn son. He played with him the entire visit. He expressed how he missed both of us and wanted to be home with us.

Although, I was very sad about the circumstances, I still loved him and wanted him to be involved with our child. I continued to go on his visitation days, until he was released early on probation after serving a year and a half on a three-year sentence due to good behavior. By the time he was released, my son was a one-year-old.

Being that he had had a roommate, my boyfriend was able to go back to his apartment where he had been residing before his arrest. In the meantime, he began to look for jobs to get things going again.

I also went back to work at Sears, and a family member kept our baby. While at work, the woman with the other baby came back again. She filed for child support against my boyfriend, which led him to request DNA testing for this child. When the test results came back, it showed that it was his child.

I wept and hurt. I felt betrayed, deceived, and lied to. This was an extremely difficult situation for me to process. I kept saying to myself, *How can a person love you and do such a thing.* I stayed very quiet and kept to myself while trying to focus on being a mother to my child.

In the meantime, I could not accept this other child because I could not deal with this along with the level of pain in my heart. I had not processed the pain, so seeing the other child would have made things even worse.

In the meantime, child-support court papers came. I attended the court proceedings with my boyfriend. Feeling very angry and frustrated, I sat quietly with him in the waiting room of the court. Before they called his name to address his case, I noticed that the other mothers were sitting in the room waiting for their cases to also be called. I felt so embarrassed, angry, and frustrated. I felt I had been forced into a large circle of problems that I knew nothing about.

After he came out of the court proceedings, the different mothers began talking to each other about him. I was so disappointed. As we rode home, he kept saying that he was sorry and tried to explain. Repeatedly, he asked me not to leave him. I remained quiet, not knowing what to even say anymore. I just began to weep. All the pain and disappointment I was going through was hard to process.

Despite it all, I tried to live my life and take care of my baby. Sometimes, we would get his oldest son on the weekend. He played football at a local park, and the mother of the child born during our relationship would also come out to the park to watch the games. Whenever we would discuss the situation regarding this child, I began to feel very angry all over again.

He did not allow any disrespect toward me. He kept saying he did not want to lose me. As time went along, we continued our ups and downs regarding this process. I still loved him, so with restrictions implemented regarding this situation, I still stuck by his side. Through the circumstances, we continued dating.

One night, he was riding with his nephew in a car. For some reason, they were stopped by police. The police began to search the car. My boyfriend was unaware of the illegal substance his nephew had on him, and he was arrested along with his nephew. As a result, he violated his probation and had to serve the remaining year and a half in prison.

Although, I had been residing with my mother, I was left alone again, trying to raise my son without his father. I continued the same cycle of visiting him in jail and waiting for him to get out so we could be together. Yes, I waited for him again, and we resumed our relationship. While incarcerated, I brought our son to visit him, and he responded as if he did not really know him. My boyfriend told me that at that time, our son's response to him had hurt him and had made him want to change his life and do better.

In the meantime, I searched daily for a job. I did not want to live off the system. I was determined to find a job. I continued going to church, prayed, and asked God to bless me with a good job so that I would be able to take care of my son. I looked every day from 8:00 a.m. to 5:00 p.m. I went to the labor department, looked up jobs, and went on interviews. Sometimes I went to three or four interviews a day. I was so desperate for a job, I even took one selling perfume on the streets for a company. This was not what I wanted. I took it because I refused to live off the system. With this job being commission based only, I did not make enough money to support my baby and me.

I went back to the labor force and began looking and interviewing at different places. I went through a program in Florida that taught us how to prepare for interviews and how to follow up after them. I did this regularly and prayed.

One night, I wrote a letter to God and placed it under my mattress. I asked God to help me find a good job with benefits and then I would pay tithes. Sure enough, the next day, I got a phone call from the police department to work as a bookkeeper. I started this job but was not happy with it. The job's duties turned out to be different from what was discussed during the interview, so I began to feel frustrated.

I went home and prayed again. After I prayed, I was led to go and listen to the messages on the answering machine. There was a message about a job with the post office, which I currently hold. I began to weep with joy and thankfulness unto God. Although I was not living in the ways of the Lord, I had been taught to pray and to trust God. I still believed in God and kept attending church services every Sunday.

In the meantime, I worked, put my son in day care, and continued to reside with my mother for a little while longer. As things progressed, I ended up getting my own apartment and my own car, which my boyfriend had helped me with before he had been arrested.

As time went on, things began to get very hard to maintain financially. My son's day care expenses became overwhelming, so I had to move him from a nice day care to one that was not so nice. I was not happy with this situation at all. I began to feel sad again. I expressed my worries to my boyfriend. At some point, he was placed in a work-release program where he repaired motorcycles at a shop. He received tips and gave them to me to help with our son's day care. Therefore, I was able to move him back to a better day care.

After he had served the remainder of his time, I made another wrong decision and let him move in with me. Even though I had been raised this way and had been instructed not to shack up, I did it anyway. As a result, I continued to suffer in the relationship. He started off doing well about being home with us. However, eventually, he turned back to his same old routine.

He started cheating again. I would go to work and come home. I would find phone numbers and other signs of unfaithfulness. We argued all the time, which was not good for my son. Our son was about two years old.

Eventually, I ended up pregnant with my second child. I carried this child with much frustration and disappointment. I ended up on bed rest due to complications with my pregnancy. I also ended up in the hospital for two weeks because my cervix began to open earlier than it should have. Even though I was dealing with these health issues, my boyfriend continued to lie and to cheat. I felt that he took advantage of the things I continued to allow. I accepted the things he did and continued with the relationship.

One day, I got tired and asked him to get out of my apartment. I repeatedly asked him to leave, but he would not do it. He was drinking heavily again and left the house to go out with his friends. He stayed out all night and tried coming back in the house. I had locked the door and had put the chain across the top.

When I got up the next morning, he was sitting up asleep on my couch. I looked at the door and found that he had gotten the wire cutters, cut the iron chain from the door and used his key to unlock the bottom lock. On another occasion, I called the police, and they came in to escort him out of the apartment. He left the apartment, but as soon as the police left, he came back and remained on the couch.

When the time came for me to renew the lease, I told him he had to go because I was not renewing it. I no longer wanted to stay with him. Things got so bad, I left him in the apartment and began looking for other places to live. I almost bought a villa but said to myself, *If I buy this place, he will find out where I live. Because I still care for him, I might let him come in.*

So, I called my mother and asked her if I could come live with her for a little while, and she said yes. I moved in with my mother because I knew my boyfriend could not come and force his way in to live with me there.

As I began living with my mom, he threatened to keep my oldest son away from me, so I let him keep him, knowing that he couldn't handle this responsibility for long. However, I felt he did this just so that he could keep in contact with me. So, there I was pregnant and dealing with all these problems. Nevertheless, I tried to make the best of things and to live my life.

My boyfriend called almost every day, promising to do better and asking me not to leave him. I told him I needed time for myself and to think things through. He never let me have that time. When I tried to ignore him, he came to my mother's house.

Late one night, he bumped my car and set the alarm off so that I would come outside. He kept knocking on the front door until my mom asked me if I wanted her to call the police. I replied that I didn't. I would just go out and see what he wanted so he would leave. Again, he asked me to give him another chance and said that he wanted his family. He also promised to do the right thing. Once again, I told him that we could see each other but that I would remain living with my mother.

At some point, my lease to the apartment ended, and we had to come together to put things in storage. While I remained living with my mother, he decided to live in his sister's house with his nephews because she had bought another home. We continued dating and waiting for the arrival of our new child. He worked at a tire place, and I worked at my job.

Sure enough, he soon started going and hanging out with a coworker. Because I was pregnant, I stayed home a lot with my mother and son. I continued going to church every Sunday and tried to get through all my past hurts.

My boyfriend and I spent a lot of time together, and I thought things were going well. At this point, he promised to do the right thing, said he wanted his family, and asked me to marry him. I accepted his marriage proposal. I felt it was a chance for us to make it together after all.

In the meantime, he got a second job with the intention of saving up for our wedding. On his days off, I expected him to spend time with his family, but he began hanging out with a coworker. When he went out with his friends, I did not trust him, so I began to question everywhere he went. I was not sure if he was being unfaithful, but I felt he was. However, I tried to remain calm because I was pregnant.

As the time came closer for me to have my baby, his family members called him and told him that I was in labor, so he rushed to the hospital and was there throughout the arrival of our new baby girl. Again, he wanted to name her, so I let him use his name as her middle name. He was very much involved with my labor and delivery, as well as the aftercare. He seemed very happy about our new arrival.

Afterward, I went back home to live with my mother who helped me with the care of my baby girl along with my son. I resided with my mother, and he resided in his sister's home. He continued to work the two jobs, and we continued to plan for our wedding. We saved our money and began to make all the arrangements concerning our wedding.

We both went to church, and I felt we were finally a family again. My fiancé prayed and asked God to bless him with a good job so that he could work one job and be faithful in his church attending, as well as spending time with his family. God granted his request, and my fiancé got a good job with the city of Greenville, which included benefits. Again, everything appeared to be going well.

I also went to look at several new property developments that were going up in different neighborhoods. I found an area that I really liked, so I proceeded to go in and complete the paperwork for the new home. I picked out the lot and began the preapproval process by myself, as I was not yet married. Once everything was approved, they began building my home, but the building process took longer than I had expected.

In the meantime, we set a wedding date and worked toward having everything ready by that date. I worked with my bridesmaids, and he worked with his groomsmen. We both seemed to be happy. My son was about five, and my daughter was about two.

Finally, the wedding arrived. We got married, left for the honeymoon, and then came back to reside with my mother while we waited for our house to be built. Now we lived as husband and wife. We spent much time together, and I felt happy. We got saved and faithfully attended a church as well.

While waiting for the completion of our home, the mother of my boyfriend's other two children became ill and eventually passed away. We ended up going to court for custody of the two children. We had to undergo home studies and visitations. We worked together to try to make them feel as comfortable as possible. We went through this process for over a year. With many difficulties and as other problems surfaced with the other parties involved, we continued to visit the kids. We wanted the children to be happy, so we all eventually came to an agreement.

About two or three years went by, and my husband started behaving as if there was something wrong. He seemed to carry a great deal of stress for a reason I was unaware of. He also seemed like he was not happy but never revealed what was wrong. He started losing a lot of weight from the stress. He became uptight and short-tempered about things that just did not make sense.

During this time, my son played football. He was about seven, and my daughter was about three. We often went out to the football field for practices and games. My husband became a football coach for my son's team, so he was there daily.

In the meantime, I noticed my husband would leave earlier than normal, so I thought he was going to work. He would also come home late sometimes. Because he was a truck driver, this was a possibility, so I didn't worry about it too much.

However, one night, I dreamed that there was a woman saying she had two children from him. When I awoke, I told him the dream and then asked him if it was true, and of course, he denied it. I then said to him, "If you did do this, then you are stupid, and I will not stay with you," so he constantly denied it.

I began to watch his behavior. We continued to go to our son's games even though I felt uncomfortable because my boyfriend continued to show stressful and nervous behaviors.

About three years into our marriage, I received a phone call from this woman who stated that she had two children by my husband. I got off the phone and told him about the call. I knew he was lying when he answered, so I said, "I am not staying with you." His eyes filled with tears, and I told him to tell the truth.

After hours of questioning, he confessed to an affair with this person but continued to deny that they were his children. I asked him many questions that included why and how he could do this to me again. I told him that there was no way I could stay with him.

I broke down crying, was angry, and wanted to tell him to get out. I advised him to stay away from me, so he slept in another room.

I will not go into the details of everything that took place in that situation, but the woman involved was not innocent either. She knew he was married but obviously did not care.

I was very angry, hurt, and confused. I felt deceived. I would have never married this man had I known all of this. I kept telling myself, *I cannot believe he married me while hiding all these secrets.* I felt my entire marriage had been based on a lie. Here I was with all this to process again, hurt on top of hurt and pain on top of pain. In my mind, I did the math. This woman had to have had one of her children the same week of my marriage and another child two years into our marriage.

We continued to reside with my mother, but I advised him to continue to sleep in another room. I did not want him to touch me at all. I wanted an annulment. However, my mother told me that she knew how I felt but that she did not want me to decide while I was angry. I was in tears and cried throughout the night. My husband did as well. We were advised to seek Christian counseling, which we did together.

Every day, he apologized and asked me not to divorce him. He said that he would do anything for me to stay with him and repeatedly asked me not to leave him. As I cried, he tried to embrace me, but I didn't even want him touching me. I kept telling him that I wanted a divorce and that I would not have married him had I known that he had done such a thing. This was a very painful process.

Eventually, court papers came to his mother's home. He underwent blood testing for both children. When the test results came back, they both turned out to be his children.

When he came to my mother's house, he showed me the paperwork. I immediately felt much anger and hurt all over again. I kept asking him why and told him that it was not fair to me. We continued to sleep in separate rooms. He knew that our marriage was in a great deal of trouble.

In the meantime, my house became ready for us to move in. I

told him he could not move in with me and bring all that baggage. He then began telling me that he would wait and do whatever it took to save his marriage. I could never understand why he would allow this type of behavior to go on for no reason. I went ahead and moved into my new house with my children. I was excited about my new space but brokenhearted about my marriage.

A court date was scheduled for child support. I went to court with him as well. While sitting there, the other mother came in with her coworkers and tried to speak to me. I ignored her as if she did not exist. They were called to go in to the court proceedings, and when they came out, she was celebrating and bragging about how much he had to pay her. I became angry and said, "he will be appealing the decision because there are other children to consider."

She then got on the elevator with her coworkers while still talking to them. We caught the next elevator. I remained silent all the way to my car. When we finally arrived home, I broke down in tears again. He held me in his arms and apologized so many times. I asked him again, "Why did you marry me like this, knowing everything you were doing behind my back?"

He replied that he did not want to lose me and that it was never his intention to hurt me. I told him that he had not been fair. He hadn't given me the chance to say if I wanted to deal with the situation or not because he had already known that I would not have married him. He continued to embrace me as I cried. I repeatedly told him not to touch me. I was so angry with him.

Every Sunday, my children and I went to church with my mother. I cried out to God at the altar, just about every Sunday. There was so much pain that I did not know how to process. I knew I needed to get into the presence of God. That way, I would not feel all the pain, hurt, and disappointment. I was usually the only one during worship service who was crying out at the altar. As soon as church was over, I would get in my car and go home. I had very little fellowship. I only spoke to whoever crossed my path on the way out the door. My personal life was completely shut down.

My husband then received another court date for the modification of the previous court order. I went to court with him again, and the women from all the other cases were there as well. We sat at a distance from them. I felt very hurt and sad but did not show it. I would have never knowingly committed such an act with another man who was in a relationship with someone or was married. These women knew that my husband had been in a relationship and had been married but had not cared.

Nonetheless, I remained quiet and waited for them to call his name. As he was called into the court proceedings, I remained outside and tried to read a magazine. After it was over, the women came out before he did with much talking. He eventually came out later. We did not discuss anything until we got in the car. He told me how each case had been separated. The last mother with the two children had not received the original amount she had bragged about, as it had been reduced.

After we got home, I was still very sad. I did not have anyone that I trusted to talk with, so I kept everything bottled up inside. I tried to continue with my life and focus on my children. I still did not allow my boyfriend to touch me. While at work, I kept to myself and pretended to be happy. I revealed nothing to anyone at my job. We did get Christian counseling and decided to try to work out our marriage because the ministry I was in did not agree with divorces. So, we remained in an unhappy and unhealthy marriage. At one point, my husband said to me, "You can't divorce me," as he reminded me of the scripture in **Romans 7:2–3, which says,**

"For the woman which hath a husband is bound by the law to *her* husband so long as he liveth: but if the husband be dead, she is loosed from the law of the husband. So then if, while *her* husband liveth, she shall be called an adulteress: but if her husband be dead, she is free from *that* law; so that she is no adulteress, though she be married to another man" (KJV).

With this in mind, I stayed angry, and it took me much longer to forgive him. I felt trapped.

CHAPTER 6

Trapped in the Wrong Relationship

As we went on in our marriage, the last mother with the two kids continued to be a problem. On one occasion, she followed me, and I called the police, who advised me to file harassment charges. I did file a report, we went to court, and she was warned and advised that if it continued, a restraining order would be implemented.

Because of her actions, it took me a long time to forgive her and let go of the things she did as well. As I told my husband what had happened, he got angry with this individual and mentioned retaliation. After the trauma, she had put me through, I told him not to retaliate but to just let it go.

I continued going to church and praying. By this time, I had given my life to Christ and had begun to seek his face in this matter. After a while, I eventually forgave my husband, and we came together again. After that, I got pregnant with my third and last child. Despite the circumstances, we tried to make it work again. I almost felt like I had no other choice because of our beliefs concerning marriage.

We both went to church together again, and my husband recommitted his life to Christ as well. I was still trying to find a way to process all of this, even though I was afraid to let go of my love for him and did not trust him. So, I just went along with the marriage. He became faithful in his church going, and I began to feel as if he was really trying to straighten up and do better for our family. We continued going to church and praying together as a family.

I was overjoyed at his help with our newborn and our other children. During the night, he would get up and check on our newborn child while I slept. I would wake up in the mornings and find him with our newborn lying on his chest, both were asleep. I was glad to see him bonding with our child. He did everything he was supposed to do during this time, so it might work. I slowly began to accept things for what they were. He had a pretty good job, was working every day, and was providing for our family. I was finally starting to feel complete.

However, when the child support orders came in, he became very frustrated and aggravated. He often said he had to take care of his family, so he began trying to figure out how he could make enough money to meet the requirements of child support and provide for his family. Therefore, he continued to go back and forth to court, attempting to get the support orders modified to a fair-share amount for each case.

While working at his first job, he began to hustle to make money on the side. I was completely against this decision because it was not a smart choice. No, it was not drug related, but he was now working two jobs, which led him to spending less time with God and our family. He slowly drifted away from church and fell into a backslidden state. Of course, the problems within the family started up again.

I continued praying every day and reading the Word of God, along with attending church with my children every Sunday. However, we all began to feel his absence, and this led to our children acting out.

Things progressively worsened to the point where everyone went into their own rooms when they came home. All communication in our home had ceased to exist. Everyone began dealing with their problems in their own ways. I, as the mother, continued to do the best I could by talking to my children, praying, and fasting.

However, my children were tired of seeing me suffer and unhappy. This led to them too becoming very angry and upset with their father.

As years went by, our children got older and began to understand things as their father continued his behaviors and was hardly home throughout the day. I stayed in a very sad place for years during this marriage.

I began to seek help, as the ministry I was in at the time, believed that you should not leave your marriage and that once you were married, you stayed married no matter what. So, I sought outside help and sought counseling. However, I found that counseling did not help me because though I felt I deserved to be treated better in the relationship, I could not get my mind to say, *I want out of this marriage.* So, I stayed in it, and it became very depressing.

I made several attempts to talk to my husband about the problems and how I felt. He was not able to say the things I needed to help me heal. In addition to this, my grandmother passed away around the same time all of this was going on. Now, I had to also process this without revealing everything I was going through to anyone. The pain I was carrying became twice as heavy. I never revealed to anyone what was going on in my marriage or my personal life because I did not trust anyone. I asked myself, how I was supposed to process so much pain.

While trying to prepare for the funeral of my grandmother, I mourned very deeply because it was my grandmother who had helped me through the loss of my father. She had often taken me to church and had prayed for me and over me frequently.

I could not even go to the previewing, as it was too much for me to bear. When it came time for the funeral, I could not even look. There was just too much pain, along with the other unprocessed pain from my marriage. As I walked by, I experienced an anxiety attack and began to have shortness of breath. I was taken to the back of the church. The pain was so deep, I did not know how to deal with it. After the funeral limo ride and the arrival at the cemetery,

I could not even get out. I wept heavily. No one knew the extent of the pain I felt that day. Others were mourning as well. I went back to her house and lay in her bed with tears constantly flowing. I tried to calm down as different family members came in to comfort me. This was a very hard day to get through. I mourned for many days.

As I tried to go on with my life, I thought about her daily. One day, I was in the kitchen talking to my mother and said to her, "You know we must love everybody." I made up in my mind that day that I needed to recommit my life to Christ. Yes, I had been brought up in church, but had not always made the right decisions in my walk with Christ. I needed to repent, confess, and accept Jesus Christ as my Lord and Savior.

On that following Sunday, I gave my life to Christ. I continued going to church, even though I was very sad, and went to the altar, crying out to God and getting in his presence I just did not want to feel the pain anymore. I did not care who saw me or what they thought of me. I just wanted to be free from this level of pain and suffering.

During this period, I would go home, and my husband would try to comfort me. I did not even know what to think about him because I was still very angry with him. I took everything one day at a time and continued to pray each day.

After about six months, my grandmother's son, who was my uncle, had a massive heart attack because he had a very difficult time processing her passing. I happened to be on the phone with my brother's girlfriend, and she mentioned that my uncle was found dead.

I said, "Who?"

When she realized that I did not know what had happened, she said, "Sorry. I thought you knew."

I called another family member to see what had happened, and sure enough, this news was true. I became very sad all over again and began crying. I tried to get myself together so that I could go out to the football field and tell my mother. Now she had lost a mother and a brother.

As I went to the football field, I was very sad. My sister was also at the football field with my mother, watching my nephew play. The closer I got to them, the more they knew something was wrong. I whispered in my oldest sister's ear what had happened, in hopes that she could tell my mother, but she burst into tears, so I had to tell my mother. She grabbed her head and said "No! No!" We left the football field and went to my mother's house.

My mother went with my older brother to my uncle's home to find out what had happened. I stayed home because I just could not take any more. I prayed and asked God for strength for my family and me. When we were preparing for his funeral, I could not say a word as we tried to get through those tough times. We were still trying to get through the loss of my grandmother and then this had happened. After the funeral, my family remained close and tried to help one another with the process. Most of us looked to God for strength.

I stayed quiet about the things that I continued to endure in my marriage as my husband continued his same behaviors. I stayed in a place of prayer and became involved in activities in church. In the meantime, the Lord began to deal with me about ministry. I became the youth Bible study teacher. I taught a foundational study of the Word of God. As God continued to reveal things to me, I began to focus on what God was doing in my life, despite the hurt and pain.

Sure enough, the enemy continued to use my husband in lies, unfaithfulness, and deceitfulness. The level of anger, regret, disappointment, and bitterness increased in me regarding my husband. I shut completely down. His behavior was unexplainable. I continued to seek God's face and to work hard toward my prayer life and relationship with God. While my husband continued his behavior, I started to read and pray more and more each day.

On one of our anniversaries, we decided to go to a marital conference in New Jersey. We really enjoyed the conference because there were married couples on a panel with different issues. One of the couples shared about an affair that the husband had, but no children had been involved.

After the discussion, the different speakers on the panel had tables set up in the lobby with their books and CDs. I went over to the table and met the wife of this couple. We began to talk, and I shared with her how I had experienced the same thing, only worse. I asked her, "How do you forgive this? How do you forgive the other woman who was involved and knew he was a married man?" She looked at me, and instead of responding to me, she gave me a strange look, which caused us both to laugh.

I knew that I was in a process where I would have to forgive, but I also had to heal from the hurt so that I could forgive. I remained quiet as my husband and I went back up to our hotel room after that service. We began to talk, and he opened-up about different things that had taken place in his childhood. We also talked about our experiences with the different level of praise at the conference. We had never seen people pursue God so hard like that in a conference. It was at an entirely different level. We had both needed that so much.

We began to weep. He apologized and held me tight in his arms. He told me he was going to get help and was ready to change his life. As we came back to Florida, he was very happy about his experience at the conference. We went to church that following Tuesday night, and he testified about his experience. However, it was not received well because the organization we were in did not feel that you should go to different ministries.

My husband felt disappointed by their response. We talked about it, went home, and continued to try to get through the process together.

In the meantime, the two children of the mother that passed away ended up coming to live with us. They needed our love and support. Despite all the problems I was dealing with, I tried to help them through the grieving process of their mother. I would tell my husband, "You are their living parent and need to spend much time with them." He made several attempts. This was a very difficult process as well. As they got older, they eventually went their own ways. We still communicate today and have a good relationship with them.

However, the problems with the other children continued to surface, and every time a situation came up, I was mad all over again. The anger came back again along with the hurt. My husband would try to comfort me, but I was so angry at him. I can say that he did not let the mothers of the other children disrespect me. The mother of the last two often tried to speak to me. I did not respond. I acted like she never even opened her mouth. I handled the situation as if she did not exist to me.

Yes, my husband had been wrong and had had no business being there with her, but I also felt that he could not have gone any further than she had allowed. I felt she had been at fault as well because it took two people to make a child, and she had known he had been married.

So, I was mad at them as well because they both had known that he had been in a relationship and had been married but just simply had not cared. Most of my anger was toward my husband because he should never have gone to either one of them. I was angry as all this circled inside my head.

Eventually, my husband started up his same behavior again. So, I stayed in an angry and bitter place with him. At times, I found myself frustrated and depressed.

I ended up getting prescribed high blood pressure medication and having a great deal of problems with my memory. I was forgetting things. It was as if my short-term and long-term memory was affected. I had two abnormal MRIs of the brain. As a result, I had to withdraw from college in my junior year. I was trying to earn my bachelor of science degree.

In addition to this, I ended up having to get a total of ten allergy shots. I was allergic to things inside and outside of the house. My husband was so off balance that he stopped maintaining the outside of the house, such as the lawn, so I started to mow it. I found myself taking care of the inside and outside of the house, which is how I developed allergies. The allergies forced me to stop maintaining the lawn, so I hired a landscaper.

My husband felt uncomfortable about me hiring the landscaper, so he told him not to come back and that he would mow his own lawn. However, he never did, so I hired an older landscaper, and he mowed the lawn faithfully.

Despite everything that was going on, I began trying to take my own health care seriously. I was under a great deal of stress, mentally, emotionally, and physically.

One day as I was working on something at home, I received a phone call from my cousin. She was crying and said, "Hurry up and get down here. Our uncle was shot in the head!" I immediately lost it. I called my pastor and tried to tell him what was going on, but it was hard to speak because I was crying. They had said my uncle had passed away.

By the time I got there, the streets had been blocked off. I went through his yard and into my grandmother's and got up close to where he was lying covered up on the ground.

I felt like everything in me had left. I felt almost lifeless. I just could not deal with this level of pain anymore. I wept and wept and wept while I hugged my mother because this was her younger brother. I wanted to get him off the ground so badly. There was much in my head and heart. I could not handle this pain. I felt as if I was at my breaking point.

My uncle had been very close to his family and had tried to keep all of us together after the passing of my grandmother. This was a deep time of mourning for my entire family.

My uncle's passing had been very unexpected, and we had a hard time trying to process it. I now had this added on top of everything else. I was walking around, but everything in my mind was stuck and unprocessed. I asked myself, *how does a person handle all this trauma and pain?*

As we went on day by day, making funeral arrangements, the hurt, the disappointment, and the anger continued to increase in me. I was so mad and confused as to why the young man had shot him. My uncle had been ministering for about ten years. He had left his past life and had turned to God, so I just did not understand this situation.

After the funeral, I still mourned hard for a long time. I spoke to my cousin who was also an evangelist. She encouraged me by sharing about the loss of her father. She then told me to fast for three days. I took her advice and fasted three days, asking God to strengthen me and lift the burden of carrying his passing off my heart. It had become too much for me along with everything else.

As I went to work, I lead a group of people, so I had to try to keep a pleasant attitude while still mourning and being confused at the same time. Finally, I asked God to help me with this. I asked God to give me closure over what had happened and to take it off my heart. God answered my prayers and did just that.

After this, I began to slowly move forward with my life, but I often still think of my uncle at times. He will forever be in our hearts.

I continued to take it one day at a time while the environment at home remained tense. After about a year, we lost a cousin who had been sick in the hospital. Then about six months later, I lost another cousin who was around the age of eighteen. While in college, she had gotten sick and had passed away unexpectedly. She had not only been my cousin but had also been my neighbor. This was just unbearable for me, so I could not even go down the street to give my condolences, even though this was her mother's only child.

After experiencing so many deaths of my loved ones along with the unprocessed problems in my marriage, I fell into a depressed state. I really did not know what to do at that point. I found myself experiencing symptoms of depression. I would go through crying spells, sadness, mood swings, memory loss, confusion, shortness of breath from anxiety, panic attacks, isolation, and disorientation. I began to see my treating physician on a regular basis. He put me on high blood pressure pills along with water pills. I was under a great amount of stress and felt as if I had no control over my body anymore.

The only thing I seemed to able to perform was my job, maybe because the duties were repetitious. In addition, I was referred to a neurologist because of my memory loss problems. The neurologist recommended that I begin seeing a psychiatrist, with plans to proceed with mental health medications and treatments. I did not want to be on mental health or any more medications.

As years went by, I did what I knew how to do, and that was to pray, read the Word of God, and continue to seek God's face. Despite the problems I was having, I began to be obedient in teaching the Word of God. The more I was faithful in teaching the foundational study class, the more God began to reveal many things to me, although I lacked understanding at the time. I noticed that God would show me things before they happened. I did not understand this prophetic gift in my life, but I knew there was something different about me. I began to have experiences with God where he would answer my prayers instantly.

The Lord showed me a picture of a woman of God, but I did not know why. I often saw her in dreams whenever I felt as if I did not know where to turn with my problems or what to do next.

I felt that I had no one to turn to who would understand the place I was physically and spiritually in. So, I remained stagnant due to a lack of understanding.

CHAPTER 7

Finding a Way Out

I continued to teach youth Bible study as I prayed and trusted God. I felt stuck and alone. I did not know what else to do. I also continued to struggle with fear. I had been called to preach the gospel. When the time for me to minister came, I would get nervous and struggle with releasing myself for God to use me. I did not know how to do this.

In the meantime, the Lord continued to show me this picture of a woman of God. I never said anything to anyone about what the Lord had been showing me because I felt no one would understand. I didn't even understand it myself.

At some point, I started visiting another church. I felt I needed more of God than what I was experiencing at the time. One night, a friend of mine invited me to a three-day revival at her church. A guest evangelist, which I had met previously, would be there. Usually, I did not attend different services, but for some reason, I went to this revival. After the second night of the revival, the evangelist and I exchanged phone numbers.

We continued to contact each other through social media and eventually met up again on several different occasions. After a few months of no contact with this evangelist, the Lord showed her to me in a dream. It was as if I had gone to sleep, had seen her, had woken up, and had gone back to sleep.

She called me the next day and invited me to a function she was having. My husband and I went down to the function and stayed throughout the service. After the service, we headed back home. Eventually, she reached out to me again and invited my daughter and me to another function, but we were unable to attend. However, the contact did not stop there. The communication with one another continued.

The evangelist invited me to church services in South Carolina. So, I began to travel from Florida to South Carolina, which was a ten-hour drive, once a month for services. As I began to attend the services, things came together for me spiritually. I felt as if I was getting what I needed spiritually.

I then started going twice a month as my husband's marital affairs continued. Once I came back from the trip to South Carolina and caught him on the phone with another woman. I immediately snatched his phone after he had quickly hung up. I grabbed him around the neck, squeezed, and said, "You put this big hole in my heart." The enemy told me to bash him in the head with an iron that was nearby, but I did not do it. I released him. At this point, I knew I had to leave before I hurt him or he hurt me.

I wasn't doing well health wise because of the overwhelming stress from the marriage, as well as the deaths in my family. My going to South Carolina provided peace and spiritual enrichment for me.

I began to seek the help of a lawyer. As I spoke with my lawyer, she told me that if I filed for a divorce, my husband could ask that I not be allowed to go more than seventy-five miles away from him with our children. So, I stayed in a place of prayer as God began to lead me in this direction.

I put in for a job transfer to South Carolina due to other reasons. I had been going back and forth between my former jobs because they had been giving me a hard time about releasing me for my transfer. It seemed as if everything was a fight, so I let it go and left it in God's hands. Then the transfer was approved. Following this, I decided to move in with a relative until I figured things out.

I continued to attend church in South Carolina. Things began to feel peaceful. We weren't arguing or fighting. Yet I remained in a very hurt, depressed, sad, confused, and mentally drained state. By this time, my oldest child had gone on to college, and my other two children resided with me. Once my husband found out that I had decided to move to South Carolina, he started complaining and saying all kinds of things that were not true. The fact remained that he did not expect me to leave, despite his unfaithfulness, because I always stayed However, this time I had had enough.

When I moved to South Carolina, I still allowed my husband to come and see the kids and me. He did not want our marriage to end. Although, I was heartbroken, I still loved my husband, so I allowed him to continue to see me as we lived apart. One thing I realized when he came was that there was hardly any arguing. We had some moments where we talked and became very emotional but didn't fight. So, we continued to try to have a marriage.

We both drove back and forth for several years to see each other. We continued to have ups and downs. Just when I felt he was changing and really wanting his family, things would surface again regarding his unfaithfulness.

At some point, I noticed that whenever we did become intimate, I began experiencing warfare with different spirits well after he had left to return home. I would be up in the middle of the night walking the floor, praying, and meditating as to what was going on, and the Lord would reveal things to me. I called my husband and talked to him. I told him the things that I was experiencing spiritually. Of course, he pretended not to know what I was talking about.

After two or three years, things continued to get worse. He started accusing me of leaving him for another man, which was not true, only to find out through a phone call that he was again involved in several affairs. One of these women was someone whom he alleged was only a business partner. In addition to this woman, he was having an affair with another one who had multiple kids from several men.

I was later told by one of these women that there were other women involved as well. She had pictures of this alleged affair. He was sitting in a car with a different woman. After hanging up the phone, I sat in the same place for a minute, telling myself that this man was not going to change or do the right thing.

I thought about the things I had endured from the marriage and decided to set boundaries along with praying, fasting, and seeking the Lord concerning the marriage. All I knew was that I wanted peace and the strength to walk away from the relationship.

When I confronted, my husband concerning the phone call I had received from the woman with multiple children, he denied it. I recapped the things that I had been experiencing spiritually whenever I had been intimate with him. I became very angry and frustrated with him because he continued to lie. The more I felt he was lying, the angrier I got. Nevertheless, after questioning him repeatedly and advising him that things were constantly being revealed to me without any phone calls, he admitted to having affairs with these women. He again claimed that they were mistakes.

I then told him it was over between us. I informed him that he was no longer welcome in my South Carolina home. I also told him that when he was in town, he would have to get a hotel because I no longer wanted him at my residence.

The next day, I called my doctor's office in tears. I made an appointment to have myself checked out. I shared with my doctor that I had only been with one partner, which had been my husband, but unfortunately, my husband had been with multiple women. I wanted to get checked thoroughly out to make sure that I was okay.

After this, I continued to enforce my boundaries that I had set up regarding his visits to South Carolina. I no longer wanted to see him, talk to him, or have him anywhere near me. I stayed very angry with him for quite some time while seeking the Lord. I felt I had no one that I could open-up and talk to regarding this situation without it being all over the place. I had not yet processed it myself along with other problems.

I decided to get outside Christian counseling from someone who did not know me, which ended up being a great move for me. One Saturday as I was setting up things for counseling, I was coming from the gym and received a phone call from my mother. She said that my older brother, Joe, was in the hospital and was not responding to treatment. When she had called me, my mother had not seemed to be upset because she had thought it had been related to his diabetes. However, she told me that my aunt Megan was at the hospital with my brother.

I went into my apartment and called my aunt Megan to see what his status was. When she told me that my brother was on life support and was not responding, I immediately got off the phone, fell on the floor, and started weeping and praying. After praying and crying, I called on one of the mothers, and she prayed for me and talked to me to help me calm down.

After speaking to her, a pastor called to speak with and encourage me. She told me some things to do to help calm myself down. Both the mother and the pastor continued to stay in contact with me and prayed for me, my family, and my brother.

The next morning, before I took my flight, I met with the pastor, who prayed over me and gave me an anointing cloth and oil for my brother. I then left to take my flight to Florida and prayed for strength because I did not know how I was going to handle the situation once I saw my brother in that condition.

Once I landed, my ride picked me up and took me to the hospital. The closer we got to his room, the more nervous I felt. When I finally looked in the room he was in, I saw the Lord wake him up from the coma he had been in the whole day prior to my arrival. As my brother looked out at me, I ran to his bedside and said, "Bruh, do you know who I am?" He nodded yes. I then hugged him, kissed his forehead, and said, "I believe you are going to be all right, so stay calm."

The nurse came in and said, "I cannot believe he is responding." She said that he had been responding all morning.

I said, "Thank you, Lord."

She began to talk to him, and he began to move his entire right side but could not move his left side. My brother had a very serious stroke that had affected his left side.

By this time, my mother had entered the room, and she now saw that he was awake. We began to pray and thank God. We also placed the prayer cloth under his head and anointed him and his room with the oil. As my mother prayed with him, he accepted Christ into his life.

By the next morning, the blood vessel that had burst had closed and the bleeding in his brain had stopped. However, my brother continued to have trouble with his breathing, so they had to do a tracheotomy where they inserted a tube in his throat before they removed the breathing tube from his mouth to make breathing easier. Eventually, he was stabilized and then was released to the next level of care, which was a rehabilitation facility.

He was moved from the hospital to the first facility where he had a bad experience. I flew down from South Carolina again to evaluate the situation and begin the necessary measures to have him transferred out of that facility to one that was in the hospital and was much better. Once he was finished with rehabilitation, he had to be moved to a facility where he would undergo more intensive rehabilitation with the hopes of regaining movement of his left side. They would also remove the tracheotomy tube so that he could breathe on his own.

After a while, he was still unable to regain strength on his left side, and they were unable to remove the tracheotomy tube, so he was again transferred to another facility, which was less intense. There he would continue his physical therapy to regain strength and movement on the left side. At this facility, he ended up in the hospital due to some type of infection. Once he stabilized, he did not want to go back to that same facility but wanted to go home.

After several attempts and problems with different rehabilitation facilities, we set up a room for him at my mother's house and brought him home for our family to care for him (per his request). My brother was very happy and pleased with this move because he wanted to go home and be around family. After seven months, he passed away. Although my family and I were very brokenhearted by our loss, I thank God that he allowed my brother to wake up, to know who his family was, to spend seven more months with us, and most importantly, to accept Christ into his life!

Now I had to go through another time of mourning while trying to deal with my ongoing marital problems. I began to prepare myself and prayed for God's strength to help me get through the funeral. After the funeral, I flew back to South Carolina, and my mother came back with me. We lived one day at a time and prayed each day as we went through our time of grief. My mother stayed with me for a while. The Lord strengthened and comforted us. We were thankful and grateful unto our Lord. Eventually, my mother flew back home and continued to try to move forward.

As I came back from dropping my mother off at the airport, I had to try to get through all of it on my own, even though it was hard. So, I continued to seek God each day and to pray for his strength. I then decided to seek counseling for grief with a Christian counselor. She began to counsel me through the steps of grief. We met at least twice a week or more as needed for several weeks. After talking everything out, I left feeling much better but still had moments here and there.

After I finished grief counseling, I was now ready to deal with the marital problems, which had me on overload. I then signed up again with the same counselor for marriage counseling. I was almost embarrassed to tell her what I had been through. I felt that she would say, "You should have been let this go!" However, once I began to open-up and talk about things, she began to also share similar problems she had experienced in her past marriage. I continued meeting with her twice a week or more as needed, until the burden of carrying everything in the marriage was not so heavy.

However, there were major issues I still needed to process and decisions I had to make. Sometimes, I would skip weeks of counseling because part of me still hoped my husband would give his life back to Christ and change so we could be a family, even though I knew he was having affairs. At one point, I stopped going to counseling. After hoping, waiting, and praying, he still didn't change. The same words kept coming out of his mouth, but no actions matched what he was saying.

I had previously told him that I would not go through another year of this. On January 15, 2016, I decided to file for a divorce and let things completely go. I also asked him to leave my home in Florida so I could let it go and move on with my life. He refused to leave. At this point, our house became an issue. At first, I continued to go back and forth with him about this home until the situation became too much of a distraction for me. This had been my first home, and I had many memories of each of my children growing up in the house and of my neighbors and friends in that area. So, to lose it all would be very painful. Nevertheless, he continued to pursue me with the same lies, stating that he loved me and still wanted his marriage and family.

I felt myself grow stronger as I began to let go of the house. The more my husband said and did to hurt me, the more I prayed and cried out to God, who strengthened me. I felt so disrespected by all my husband's actions. The Lord revealed to me several events that had taken place in my house. When I again confronted my husband, he denied the events. The more I tried to put the house behind me, to forget about it, and to live my life, the more the problems continued to arise. So, this was a matter I could not just ignore.

I continued to fast, to pray, and to seek God regarding this matter so that this would no longer be a distraction for me. Eventually, I got to a place of no longer caring about the house and asked the Lord to take it off my heart. I believed that just as the Lord had blessed me with this home, he would give me another home. I had to change my way of thinking and to trust the Word of the Lord. The Lord gave me strength, and I gradually began to let go of the house.

CHAPTER 8

The Process of Letting Go

Although, I was brokenhearted, I began the process of letting go. I believe that acceptance was the beginning of this process. Letting go was the hardest thing for me in this marriage/relationship. Even though the average person would have said enough is enough, I still had hope and held onto my marriage. I still prayed for him and wanted him to change and turn to God. However, he was not ready. I had to go through this process of letting go so that I could let God have his way.

During the process, I continued calling my husband and had constant contact with him. I would also stay on the phone with him while he fell asleep just to make sure no one else called him or came to our home. During the night, he would wake up and realize we had fallen asleep while talking on the phone and would hang it up. We would call each other back once we were both awake and talk about the night before. Every day, we spoke to each other. Of course, we continued to argue concerning his unfaithfulness, lies, betrayal, deceitfulness, adultery, lust, and mind manipulation.

On one occasion, he came to visit, and I stopped by his hotel before he had to leave early the next morning. While I was lying on the couch, I saw the light on his phone come on after he had dozed back to sleep. I went over and answered the phone, and of course, the person he had claimed he was no longer having an affair with was calling. I talked to and eventually hung up on this individual.

Again, I became angry at his lies and deceit and began arguing with him and pushing him. I was so angry, I said, "Let me back up from this man before I hurt him." At that moment, I repented for anything that I had said or done that may have been offensive because nothing was more important to me than my relationship with God. As he checked out of the hotel and I proceeded back home, I recapped the things that had happened from past to present. Then I decided after twenty-eight years, enough was enough. I was completely done and began to seriously cut things off.

Later that year when Christmastime came, my son wanted to have a good Christmas with his father. I began communicating with my husband again, trying to set things up for Christmas because my son's mind was set on spending time with him. Although this was extremely difficult for me, I did it for my son, and he said he had a good Christmas.

As I was taking my husband back to the hotel, we began talking again. Things began to go in a direction that I was very uncomfortable with, so I left. When he called, and asked if I was coming back, I said, "No I can't." I decided I could not let myself go back to that same place again. I realized that every time I took a step forward, I ended up being knocked back to the same place I had started from.

After this, I didn't call him for the remainder of the year (the last ten days in 2016). I fasted and prayed. In the meantime, one of my daughter's friends passed away, so we had to go to Florida during the last weekend of that year.

As we approached Florida and began to set our plans for attending the wake on the night before the funeral, I stopped by my old house. Of course, my husband was not home, so my daughter called him. He informed her that he was not home. We then went to the shop where he worked and ended up seeing him in a car with the same woman who had multiple kids with him. Of course, things did not go well. I became very angry at his ongoing lies but was not surprised. I ended up leaving and helping my daughter in her situation.

After the viewing, I thought that I would never go back to that house where I knew he was waiting to talk to me. I felt as if he only wanted to use mind manipulation and come up with an excuse again, so I did not go back to that house. I would go to my mother's home and then on home from there. Of course, he called and tried to explain, but there was nothing to explain.

Early in the morning before leaving for home in South Carolina, I stopped by my old house. As I was putting the key in the door, he opened it. I went in and was immediately angry with him. There was a gift on the couch. When I asked him, who had bought the gift and if it was from one of his affairs, he stuttered and eventually said yes. This man had just spent Christmas with our children in South Carolina and then he went back to Florida and spent the New Year with the woman he had been having an affair with.

I became very angry and argued with him. I left the house very angry, but as I drove down the highway, I really began to analyze everything. Once again, I decided I wanted no more of this. I blocked all his contact numbers in my phone.

However, things did not stop there. He began to text and/or call my son's phone. I eventually had to get involved, so I unblocked him. Again, my husband tried to convince me that he wanted to work out the marriage and told me that he loved me. He did this while still being involved with his ongoing affair and other relationships as well. Finally, I said to him, "Not another year will I do this," and I meant it this time.

Although, I made up my mind to let go several times and took necessary measures to do so, I somehow ended up removing his blocks from my phone and my instant Messenger on Facebook. There were different occasions where he insisted on being involved with my son's sports events, so for my son's sake, I tried to keep my husband updated. However, as I fought and prayed to let go, matters continued to arise.

One of the women from his affairs would repeatedly end up sneaking access to his phone and reading his text messages. She would also attempt to call me, which became a major problem. On one occasion, she called me (the wife) demanding that I leave my own husband alone while claiming to be his girlfriend. I thought, *who in their right mind would call the wife and demand that she leaves her own husband alone?*

I received several phone calls and miscellaneous texts through various Google account numbers. When I would block one phone number, the woman would create another one and text again. When I confronted my husband about this, of course he pretended as if he had no clue as to what was going on. As we talked on another day, he admitted that the calls could be coming from his affair because he had seen something on her phone.

After a while, I changed my phone number. My husband also told me that he had ended his affair. Yet as time went by, I found out that he was still in this affair and was telling me the same lies. After changing my number three months later, I received another phone call while I was at work, and it was from this same woman. I asked her how she had gotten my phone number, and again, she mentioned that she got it from his phone.

After speaking with her, I hung up and immediately called him. By this time, I was very upset with him. He expressed anger toward her and told me that he was sorry and was going to fix this problem. My husband also indicated that he would pay to get my number changed for me again. My husband even went as far as to fly up to South Carolina, to meet with our kids, and to ask them to forgive him. He said that he wanted to work things out with the marriage and our family. My kids, one at a time, told him how they felt about him and his affairs. They were very angry with him. He promised to stop the affair, as well as others, and work on restoring his family.

After our kids and I had left the hotel, I went back home and talked to my oldest son. He did not believe my husband and asked that I not go back to where he was. I said, "Okay." I did not go back to the hotel where my husband was but instead went before God and prayed. I asked the Lord that if this was a deception to please show me. As I fell asleep on the couch, I dreamed about a big snake (deception), I immediately opened my eyes as I woke up.

I woke up and went to my son's room to talk to him, but he had left for work. I went in his room, kneeled, and prayed. After I prayed and tried to lie back down to sleep, my telephone rang, and I heard someone saying, "Your husband took my phone and busted my window last night."

I kept saying, "Who is this?" but she wouldn't say her name. Finally, I recognized her voice. I became angry with my husband because he had been on the phone with me until about midnight. I could see now that mind manipulation, lies, and deceit continued to operate in this man.

Guess what. He went back to Florida and continued having this same affair, as well as other adulterous behaviors. So, I called him to find out what was going on. I told him about the phone call I had received. He of course denied having her phone. Surprisingly, her phone rang while he was on the phone with me. I said to him, "You are lying. I just heard another phone ring. So why do you have her phone?"

He then explained that she had called him to come to a club, so he had gotten up and had gone to the club. Apparently, they had gotten into a disagreement, which had escalated to her calling me. Nevertheless, this was none of my concern at that time. I was just tired of all the lies and chaos associated with that man.

After this event, I received a phone call from a family member who had been waiting for my husband. My husband had said that he would take him to a car mechanic he knew. When my husband had shown up, he had been driving the woman in the affair's car. My husband had no clue that this individual had phoned me and told me the color and type of car he had been in. Of course, I confronted him. He could not deny it, so instead, he got mad and found a reason to get off the phone. At that point, I realized that this man had no problem lying, not even to his own children.

I began to shut things down again. I blocked my husband's

phone number and all contact with him once again. However, this type of behavior from him still did not stop. He then began to send me emails stating that he loved me and did not want to be in the affair. He went as far as to say that he did not understand why he was doing these things. I explained to him as best I could that because of demonic attacks and seducing spirits, he was being used to make wrong decisions, such as backsliding, watching porn, committing adultery, and disobeying. He had opened the door for these spirits to come in.

It seemed that the more I tried to minister to him, pray for him, and give him the Word of God, the less he listened. I still hoped he would change, so I continued to pray for him and asked the Lord to save and deliver him. However, I realized that my husband had free will. He had to want God for himself and not just for me. I noticed that this continued to be a repeated cycle, which led to situations that continued to cause pain, hurt, delay, frustration, disappointment, and suffering. I held on to this hope and continued to communicate with him.

The situation progressively worsened over time. I then began to see pictures of him and this same woman on social medial where she posted a picture of my husband with her and added a caption that said, "true love." Of course, I told him about this picture a couple of days later, and he said he had asked her to take the picture down. Once I had seen the picture, I had said to myself that the devil was bold at what he did. This did not bother me emotionally, but I became a little angry with him because of the disrespect that was shown to his children and marriage. I could not understand why he had allowed himself to get tangled up with this woman who had seven kids of her own from four different men. None of the children were his. This just did not make any kind of sense. I was very angry with that he would even be involved in this type of affair.

Finally, one Saturday after having a major argument with him, I called him and told him I no longer wanted to talk to him, see him, or have anything else to do with him. On that day, I blocked him again. I even changed my phone number a third time. This time, I did not give him my phone number. Eventually, I received an email from him asking me if I had changed my number. I told him I had and stated that I did not want him or the other woman to have my new number. I did not respond to any other emails from him, even though he sent another email asking me to please call him. I refused to call.

After thinking through things for a couple of days, I emailed him back and informed him that I wanted a divorce. He responded back and said that he still loved me, that he did not want the affair and would leave it, and that he did not want a divorce. He also mentioned that if I filed for the divorce, he was not going to sign it.

At first, I became very frustrated with this response. However, I decided to fast and pray for God's strength, leading, and guidance in this. The Lord gave me strength, and I continued to say that I wanted a divorce. I even bought a divorce packet and set up an appointment to speak to a lawyer regarding the matter. During everything I had gone through in this marriage, I had never come out and said, I wanted a divorce until now. I believe it was because part of me still held on to hope that he would repent, change, get saved, and seek a true relationship with God to restore his family. Yet he did not do this but chose to continue in his affairs while trying to convince me from his unclean spiritual place that he still loved me and wanted his family.

I made up in my mind during December 2016, I was no longer going to suffer through this repeated cycle of same events from this man for another year. As we entered into 2017, I informed my husband that I was not going through another year of these same events, which had been caused by him. The same events continued throughout 2017.

I began to pray and really cry out to God, and what the Lord showed me was truth. My husband continued to try to convince me that he had ended his ongoing affair and that he wanted his family. However, as I went to God regarding the matter, the Lord showed me how my husband had chosen this affair rather than living right and restoring his family. This had not happened very many times before. This came to me because the Lord had been showing me truth all the time. Due to my lack of understanding, I realized that the Lord had been showing me. The Lord opened my mind of understanding, and I saw that whenever I prayed about the things my husband said to me, the Lord would show me truth.

So, I told my husband to stop denying what the Lord had shown me and to just be quiet because it was very dangerous to deny the things of God. I continued to pray and cry out for God's strength to let go of this relationship. As a result, I began to feel the pain and the stress of this situation lessen each day. I also continued to keep my husband blocked in my phone.

I tried going on with my life again, began to take it one day at a time, and prayed each day. I felt the Lord strengthen me and help me release the situation more and more each day. I began to accept that my husband was going to lie about his situations no matter what and just to get what he wanted. I wanted to shut every open door to this. No matter how much I wanted him to change and didn't want to lose my family, I still had to conclude that his free will had to want God. I cried many nights. I could not understand how someone could say he loved and wanted his family and then did not choose God and do the right thing. Instead, he chose the other way, despite his denial. I went by his actions because his mouth said one thing while his actions showed another.

No matter how I tried blocking him on my phone, I ended up talking to him again off and on by Messenger through Facebook because of situations that involved my son. During those times, he would ask me to call, and when I called him, he began to play games back and forth with me. He tried to play both sides while denying things.

Again, my contact with him became very frustrating. I felt held up in this marriage due to his ongoing infidelity and issues involving my house. The house was in my name. I had purchased my house before we had been married. Nevertheless, he refused to move out of the house, fell behind in mortgage payments, and eventually stopped paying the mortgage altogether. I confronted him about having other women in my house. The Lord had shown me through dreams that he had had other affairs in my house in addition to the ongoing affair he remained in.

I confronted him about having women in my house, and he denied this. I explained to him that the Lord had shown me this, and he denied it. So, I became upset with him and told him that God did not lie. I asked him why he was lying. Nonetheless, I continued to fast, pray, and work on getting untied from this marriage, emotionally, physically, mentally, and spiritually.

Although I had stopped having sex with him, we were still tied together in that regard. Sometimes in my dreams, I would see images of him trying to have sex with me. I began to rebuke and cast out the sexual spirits, to plead the blood of Jesus, and to command them not to return. I would also say, "My heart belongs to the true and living God." I continued to fast, to pray, and to ask God to get rid of all my anger, resentment, retaliation, hatred, soul ties, and anything connected to the marriage that was not pleasing to him. I still did not completely cut my husband off from my communication but desired to continue moving in the direction of the divorce. At times, I found it difficult not to have contact with him due to my son being involved in sports. It seemed like the more I prayed, the worse he got.

Whenever I did allow him to talk to me, he continued telling me the same lies to try to keep me in a delayed place. I finally realized what was going on. I meant what I had said about not going through it another year. This was truly a repeated pattern of lies and deceit. I did not believe him and could not allow myself to even open-up or to consider his lies anymore. He did not present anything new. It was the same lies and deceit that kept me in this delayed place. Yet it was my fault because I allowed this type of behavior to go on. I no longer wanted to be on a roller coaster, emotionally, mentally, or physically. I was set on getting a divorce.

As I took necessary measures in this area to speak to a lawyer concerning a divorce, certain issues did arise. However, I thought, *I am going to trust God in every area because my desire is to stay clean and live holy.* I made up my mind that I did not want to live in stress and a mess, so I began to let everything go, which included my house in Florida. I remembered that the Word of God said in **Matthew 19:29, "And everyone that hath forsaken houses, or brethren, or sisters, or father, or mother, or wife, or children, or lands, for my name's sake, shall receive an hundredfold, and shall inherit everlasting life" (KJV).** With this scripture in mind, I began to step out in faith and to trust God through this process.

I took the necessary measures to speak to the representative of the bank who was assigned to my house regarding foreclosure matters. I went back and forth in my mind between trying to see if I should refinance this house or sell it. Either way, I wanted to be free from the obligation of it and from any connection with my husband. Again, prayer was the key to this problem. I continued praying and seeking the Lord.

As I was sleeping, the Lord showed me the house and all the contamination and unclean spirits that were present. The Lord also said to me, "Do not go back in there!"

I said, "Yes, Lord." From that point onward, I did not go back there. I also told my husband that he could have everything in that house and that I did not want anything out of it. So, this was clearly the answer I needed to keep moving forward with selling the house. I then called the banking representative back and asked for her help with selling the house. She gave me a few names of realtors to help me. I contacted a few of them. However, one realtor continued to contact me and ensured that she could help me. Therefore, I decided to conduct my business with her.

The realtor began to send the necessary paperwork for me to sign so that the house could be listed for sale. She began to deal back and forth with my husband and me. Since he was still in the house, she had to make him aware of the importance of moving out so that the house could be sold before the foreclosure selling date. The hardest part was trying to get my husband to cooperate and accept the fact that he had to move out of the house. When she contacted my husband, he finally had to face reality that he had to move.

In the meantime, the realtor listed the house for sale, and people began to come by and show interest in purchasing the house. Over thirteen people wanted to purchase the home within three days of listing it. While negotiating the terms and conditions of the house, my husband moved out as much as he could in the following three to four days. Once an agreement was reached with a buyer through my realtor, a date was set for closing on the house. My husband continued moving all his items up until the date of closing. The final items were removed on that day.

At closing time, we hit a few bumps here and there. We had to get my husband to sign paperwork that would allow the closing because of some shared marriage property law in Florida. After the title company explained the matters to my husband, he eventually signed the necessary paperwork. I too had to sign paperwork, which was then FedEx back. Once the final deal was made, we closed on the home.

I want to take a moment right here to thank the Lord for selling this home because nobody did this but God. My home sold within two weeks of listing it. This was God! I had gone through years of torment while trying to get out of this obligation and without it ruining my credit. I am so thankful. To God be the glory!

After this was final, there was another decision that had to be made. I was still married and hurt and was trying to decide when and how to let go of the marriage. My husband always mentioned my retirement. I had been at my job for twenty-seven years. The fact that he could take half of what I had worked so long and hard for was unbearable. He used this as a hook to keep me stuck in the marriage while he continued to go from place to place, traveling on vacations with the woman in his affair. Pictures continued to surface on social media. He had no shame about his adulterous affair. He did not care that it hurt his children when their friends saw their father with another woman.

It was even sadder that it was his own family members who were posting the pictures. There was no respect for my children and me. I just had to keep speaking to my children and encouraging them. I even advised them to unfriend the family members that were posting the pictures. I continued asking God to strengthen my children and me and to help us let go and move forward. Eventually, I got tired of the disrespect, stepped out in faith, and began the divorce process. As I mentioned previously, I spoke to many lawyers, and all of them told me all that my husband could do to me. My husband always threatened that he would request some of my retirement. He would not come straight out and say it, but he always brought the matter before us.

Because I had been on my job for twenty-seven years, I had a lot to face in this divorce. My husband used this to delay the divorce. He knew I did not want to give him half of my retirement or whatever he thought he was entitled to besides the house. There were also issues that had to be decided regarding our son, who was sixteen years old and a minor. Regardless of the matters before me, I knew I had to get out of the marriage to live a happy life because it was not healthy for my children and me.

As each day went by, I could not live with the fact that I was still married to a man who was living with another woman and off my health and dental insurance while treating her as if she was his wife. The more I thought of this, the angrier I became. I continued to seek God's face. I did not want to be angry but just wanted peace.

One day as I lay in my bed and let my thoughts flow freely, I began to think about what the lawyers had said my husband could do to me, along with the things he had already done to me. I finally thought, *I do not care what he does anymore because this cannot continue. If he takes half of my retirement, so be it! I just want to be free. If God can sell my house and free me from that obligation, then God can help free me in this divorce.* I had to trust God and proceed with the divorce. So, I read through the divorce packet and began to complete the financial packet myself. I also signed up for the four-hour mandatory parenting class the courts required because we had a minor child.

After finally completing the divorce packet, I headed downtown to file the paperwork through the courts. I must say that this was very hard and emotional, but I knew it needed to be done. As I approached the courthouse building, I began to feel more emotional but proceeded through the security checkpoint. Once I made it through this area, I went to the office to file the paperwork. I signed in, sat down, and patiently waited to be called. Finally, I heard someone say, "Mrs. Gold?"

I replied, "Yes," and the young man told me to come with him. I proceeded in that direction. He then took the paperwork, asked me a few questions, and began to scan the paperwork into the computer. After this was complete, I was given a ticket and sent to another window where I received the completed divorce packet along with another packet that had instructions that were to be served to my husband in Florida. Once I received this packet and paid my $250 filing fee, I left the building and walked back to my vehicle. My mind would not be still, and I started getting emotional. However, I kept telling myself that this had to be done and that this could not continue because I was not happy.

I drove back home with tears flowing down my face. I thought, *I cannot believe that this man has gotten himself into such a bad place spiritually that he is now blind to what the enemy is using him to do. He has lost his entire family and home.* My heart was truly heavy because we had been married for thirty years. I kept driving and thinking. Then I began to worship and praise the Lord all the way home. Once I arrived home, I called one of my mentors and told her about what had happened. She encouraged me and shared her story with me, which helped me move forward and trust God through the process.

My next step was to have my husband served with the divorce papers. The hearing was set for thirty days after I had filed the paperwork, so I had to move quickly. The next day, I went and purchased the fifty-dollar money order. This was the amount I had to pay to have him served in the state of Florida. I also had to send a picture of him in the divorce packet. There was also a return envelope enclosed so that they could send me a receipt showing that he had been served. I finally gathered everything together and headed to the post office about the third day after filing.

Once I got to the post office, I again began to feel emotional. However, I kept telling myself that it had to be done and that I could not live like this. I waited in line for a post clerk to call me. Finally, I was called and went up to the desk. I began to tell her that I needed a return receipt for the mail because it was time sensitive. She followed gave me the receipt I needed and the tracking information. The paperwork went out that day.

After about a week, I followed up. I called the county sheriff's office to see if they had received the packet. For some reason, the tracking system kept telling me it had been delayed. I did not understand this. I waited another day or so, but it continued to say the same thing. So, I called FedEx and they told me that the package was in route and on the truck. Well this had been the status for a couple of days.

I took it a step further and called the actual site where the package was supposed to be delivered and spoke to a supervisor. I explained that the material was time sensitive and had to be served due to an upcoming hearing. I also informed the supervisor that it had been two weeks and that my husband still had not been served. The supervisor apologized and placed me on hold to search for the package. After waiting on hold for about five minutes, she came back on the phone and said, "I am sorry, but the package was entered into the system wrong, and he was served today." I went online myself, and sure enough, it showed that he had been served. So, I said, "Thank you," and we hung up.

That same day, my husband texted my daughter and told her that he would have to get a lawyer because he had to go to court.

At this point, my daughter had no clue what he was talking about because she did not know he had been served.

After about two days, he texted my daughter and asked her to have me call him. I waited a long time before I finally picked up the phone to call him. Right away, he started saying that he did not want a divorce and that he had to move in with the other woman because he had no other place to go. I told him that he did have other places that he could go. A real man would find his own place to live and not live off someone else, if that really was the case.

Nonetheless, I told him it did not matter. He began to get upset, accused me of having another man, and saying that that was why I was selling the house and filing for a divorce. Of course, we argued back and forth because this was not true. I also told him he had no right to ask me anything, being that he was living with the other woman. I felt as if he was trying to have his cake and eat it too, but that was not going to happen on my end. Although I had to contact him several times concerning our son, I stayed in a place where I guarded my mind, heart, emotions, and spirit. I wanted to completely let go this time for myself and because I had had enough.

As time continued to draw near to the court date, my husband flew up to see my son's football games. At each game, he found a way to contact me or to try to be around me. During one of the games, he came and sat next to me unexpectedly and began to ask me about being together. He also asked if we could work things out. I said, "Not without God." He kept trying to be with me, but he did not want to give his life to Christ.

On another occasion, he lied and said he could not contact an Uber driver to pick him up and asked if I could take him to the hotel. Of course, I took him there, but we argued all the way to the hotel. When he got out of the car, it was almost as if I could no longer stand being around him.

In the meantime, I had to learn the pattern of and the motive behind the actions of the evil spirit. So, I began to inquire of the Lord. I prayed and prayed and prayed. I asked God for his strength over the situation and to give me wisdom. I realized there were spirits of frustration, confusion, and mind manipulation.

Now that I knew what was going on, I chose not to argue back and forth with my husband. As the pictures continued to surface, it got to the point where they did not bother me anymore because I realized that the enemy was intentionally doing things to get me upset and to take my focus and alignment off God. I continued to speak with my mentors, pastors, and counselors regarding this matter, who were also praying for me and my children. It took a great deal of time to completely let go. I had to stay before God, seeking him daily to bridle my tongue and break all ties.

Our court hearing was approaching. We were now five days away from it, and he continually tried to prevent the divorce. He would send messages through my children, asking me to call him. Sometimes I called, and sometimes I did not.

After all he had put me through, the fact that he could possibly ask for money tore my heart. He came to another one of my son's football games and found me again. I asked him about this. I said, "You really would try to take money from me like that after all you have done to me?" He just looked at me. He did not say yes or no. However, I realized that he was doing this to make me feel trapped, but I refused to stay in that place.

I also began to tell him in one of our phone conversations that we did not need lawyers but that we could work it out on our own. He then began to say, "I am coming with a lawyer. I am telling you now that I am coming with a lawyer." I realized all his actions and words were to scare me, in hopes of keeping me from moving forward with the divorce. Again, I did not let this shake me. I was determined to move forward regardless of what he said.

It was now the day before our court date. I prayed and asked the Lord to show up on my behalf, to confuse the mind of the enemy, and to change the heart of the judge to rule in my favor. As **Proverbs 21:1 says, "The king's heart *is* in the hand of the LORD, as the rivers of water: he turneth it whithersoever he will"** (KJV).

I continued to pray that night. I eventually fell asleep and woke up early the next day. I then prepared for the big day. As I began to wash my face, I started to feel some sadness but was okay because I believed that the Lord was with me. My oldest son and I got dressed, ate breakfast, and proceeded to the courthouse.

On this day, there was so much traffic on the way to the courthouse that we thought we were going to be late. Now we were rushing through traffic, trying to arrive on time for the hearing. This was a very tight and close ride. I prayed silently that they did not dismiss the case and to help us make it there safely on time. We finally arrived at the courthouse a little after my time for the hearing. I had my son drop me off in front, and then he parked the car. I rushed through the security checkpoint and asked for directions to the courtroom. I had to take the elevator upstairs to the eighth floor and finally arrived at the entrance of the courtroom where I went in and sat quietly.

I looked around the room, and my eyes landed right on my husband. He was already there, on time, and waiting. He had already checked in. So, I sat quietly waiting. Once the clerk came out and recognized that I was there, she asked my name and I replied that I was Ruth Gold. She then went back to check me in and said that she would be with me in a moment. She verified that my husband and I were there for the divorce hearing.

After we waited another thirty minutes, she called us in for our hearing. I sat on one side, and he sat on the other. The judge began to introduce herself and verified all parties involved, which was my husband and me. She spoke on the issues involved in a divorce.

She allowed my husband to speak first, and he said that we had been together for thirty years and that he did not want a divorce. Then the judge let me speak about the divorce. Right away, my husband denied being the father of the other children who had been born during the marriage. He was not truthful and said that they had been born before the marriage. I said that this was not true and that I had proof (I had the court order for child support that showed their dates of birth and the blood test).

Once this issue was established, my husband questioned a restraining order that he thought I had placed against him. Again, this had not been the case. When I tried to explain, I broke down in tears and said that there had never been a restraining order and that he had misunderstood the paperwork. The judge further explained the procedures of the restraining order and that there was no restraining order being enforced now. Based upon the evidence and testimony, the Judge decided that she would grant my divorce. She then released us to go into the waiting area to wait on mediation.

At that point, the only matters that we still needed to discuss were the financial ones. We had to go back into the courtroom to meet with the mediator to discuss child support and any other assets. While my son and I sat, and waited quietly, my soon-to-be ex-husband got up, walked across the room, and out the door. I could hear him outside on the phone talking to someone. I continued weeping because I was so hurt and disappointed about everything.

As my son and I talked quietly, my husband came back into the courtroom and sat down again. About thirty minutes later, my husband got up again, walked across the room, and went back outside the courtroom.

Suddenly, I heard my husband calling, "Ruth ... Ruth ..." Then he waved at me and asked me to come outside so he could speak to me.

So, I stepped outside and said, "What?"

He said, "Are you sure you want to do this?"

I said, "Yes."

He went on to say he did not want a divorce. He even said, "If I get my own place, can you and I be together?"

I said, "No," and then pulled out a picture that someone had sent to me of him and the other woman in Vegas. He looked stunned and asked where I had gotten the picture. I told him how I had gotten it and that he could not say a word because he was busted. I began to feel frustrated, so I walked away from him.

He asked me again as I was walking away, "Can we be together?"

I looked back and quoted the Word of God: "**Can two walk together, except they be agreed? (Amos 3:3 KJV)**. I then walked back into the courtroom and sat near my son as we waited to be called for mediation.

After about two hours of waiting, the mediator called my husband and me. Again, I sat on one side, and he sat across from me. The mediator introduced herself and explained the purpose of mediation. She went through the assets. When she asked about the house, we both replied, "It is sold." There was no problem there. She went on to ask about any retirement, and right away, he said, "She has retirement."

I then replied, "That was before I married him," which was non-marital. She then moved on to child-support issues. She asked for W-2 forms or sources of income to establish child support. I produced my check stub, and right away, my husband lied and said he was not working. I said, "He works under the table." The mediator then told him that she would like to work things out between the two of us, but if he did not produce any income then the judge would have to determine the amounts he had to pay. My husband then began to say that he made a certain amount per month.

I told the mediator that I would like him to continue paying what he had been paying per week. I was not seeking anything further because I wanted the divorce to be settled. I did not want any delays. My husband agreed to continue paying the amount he was now paying. The mediator wrote this down in the court orders, so child support was established.

The mediator then asked if there was anything else. I replied, "No." My husband then began to complain that I had changed my phone number and that he did not have any way of getting in contact with me. I said that our son had just turned sixteen years old and that my husband had his number to contact him.

My husband then complained that sometimes he tried to contact my son but could not get him because he was in practice. Sometimes there were important matters he needed to talk to me about. So, the mediator asked me why I did not want to give him my number.

I explained to her that when he was asleep, his affair went through his phone, replied to his messages, found my phone number, and called my phone, leaving all kinds of ridiculous messages. If he couldn't control his phone then he did not need my phone number.

The mediator then told him that he would need to take control of this matter because this involved his son. She then asked me if we could try to work through it and allow him to have the number. She made him agree not to call me unless it was related to my son. I agreed not to call him unless it was related to my son as well. So, I had to give him my phone numbers.

Regarding visitations, he was advised not to come unless he notified me and planned with my son prior to his visit at a mutual location. With all matters agreed upon and discussed, we were released to await the final orders from the judge. We waited at least another two hours.

Then we were called in before the same judge for the final orders. She again read out the agreements to both of us. We then signed the agreements. She read the request for the orders, and I agreed. My husband disagreed with some of the request, so I explained what I meant in the request, and he remained quiet.

At this point, the judge read out the request for the divorce and granted it. I then got up and took the copies so that I could have them filed in the court system. My now ex-husband immediately walked out of the courtroom with tears in his eyes. My son and I got on the elevator and went down to the court clerk's office to file the final orders for the divorce. I was told I had to wait two days for a gold-sealed copy.

My son and I left after we had filed the papers and proceeded to my car. After we got into the car and drove down the highway, I thought, *this is finally over. My God did it again!* After all my husband's threatening's to take my retirement money and to appear with a lawyer, God showed up on my behalf! My ex-husband was not able to get one dime from me, and he did not even have a lawyer present at the hearing. All glory belongs to our God!

Later that night as I lay down, I could not believe we had gone to court, and my ex-husband had made a promise not to contact me unless it related to my son. Can you believe the man texted me and accused me of divorcing him because I had another man? He did this a couple more times until I ended up blocking him.

As I went to work the next day, I was a little upset by his actions but unblocked him because I was trying to comply with court orders. While I was speaking to my supervisor, my ex-husband called my phone again. After I finished speaking to my supervisor, I was angry. I planned on calling him and asking him what the problem was. However, before I could do this, he called again and said that he just wanted to say he was sorry. He had not meant to aggravate me but had been sorry.

He then began to say that he did not want a divorce. I replied, "But you still do not want to straighten up and do the right thing. I love the Lord, and I want God, but that is not what you want." I then said to him, "I gave you what you chose. You are living with another woman, so she can have you, and you can have her because I am done. You were given more than enough time to do the right thing, but you still chose to do the wrong thing."

He then said, "All right, all right, but I still love you."

I said, "Okay," and we hung up. I went back to work, and every now and then, I would just thank God and say, "Nobody but you, God." God did this for me, and I was praising God at work.

After I got off work, it still had not sunk in that I was finally divorced. I continued to feel my emotions going up and down. I had been divorced on a Tuesday and had to be in another area of South Carolina for a conference on Thursday, which came at the right time for my youngest son and me. We were trying to process the after effects of the divorce. That Thursday, we both left and took a two-and-a-half-hour drive to the conference.

Once we arrived, we checked in and met with my mentor. She had been praying for me during that difficult time, so of course, she wanted to know what had happened during the court hearing. I went into my room, got my son all settled in, and relaxed until time for church. We both sat in the hotel room and talked about how we felt and how to move on with our lives. Being at the conference and around prayer warriors and positive people helped us get through that week and strengthened us to keep moving forward.

Yes, it hurt, but I felt free. Now, all I had to do was process the after effects. I had to learn how to live free!

CHAPTER 9

A New Me!

Although I was broken hearted, I began to take it one day at a time and to pray each day. I also wanted to reach my destiny, so I prayed and ask God to clean and strengthen me from my past and anything associated with my marriage. The Bible says in **Romans 8:37, "Nay, in all these *things* we are more than conquerors through him that loved us," and, in Matthew 19: 26, "But Jesus beheld them, and said unto them, With men this is impossible; but with God all things are possible" (KJV),** so I focused more on prayer, reading my Bible, hearing from God, working out, eating healthy foods, and following through with the things that would move me forward toward my destiny, such as writing this book.

I told my husband that I forgave him but refused to spend another year dealing with his behavior. As a result, I kept him blocked in my phone. I talked to my pastor, my mother, and two good Christian friends, who had my best interests in mind. These positive people kept me encouraged, prayed for me, and wished the best for me in the things that I wanted to accomplish.

I decided to let go of everything associated with my past so that I could be fully used by God because my desire had become God's will and God's way. The more I stayed in constant contact and communication with my past and focused on saving the house, the more delays and distractions there were on my way toward my destiny. So, I had to decide whether I was going to continue to waste time tangled up in this or proceed to my destiny. Therefore, I decided I would no longer let my past control my destiny.

I began to speak up and say, no more of this! I decided to take control of my own life through prayer and by God's leading. I can say today that I thank God I am experiencing a peace in my mind, spirit, and home because I let it all go. I started focusing on the things that meant more to me.

I began working out and eating healthier to make sure I stayed in good health. I became more involved with activities in church and with my children. I decided that God was my focus because he had given me the strength to come through all that I had endured. I no longer held anger, resentment, retaliation, hatred, or revenge in my heart for my ex-husband. Instead, I chose to pray that God would save and deliver him and that my ex-husband would find his way back to God.

I am more focused now on the new me in Christ Jesus. I must say that I am happy that I let go and let God take control of my life. Most importantly, I found "ME" in the midst of it all!

CHAPTER 10

Let's Look at My Process

1. How do you survive the adultery?

My answer to this question is God. I had to put my focus on the Word of God, pray, and develop a relationship with God because I found out that it was not the conversations I had with my friends that mattered but my communication with God. The more I prayed, fasted, and continued to stay before God, the stronger I got. God gave me strength over the fact that this had occurred. To begin my healing process, I had to come to the place where I accepted that it had taken place and had made a great impact on my marriage.

2. How do you process so much pain from an adulterous affair?

There was much pain from the beginning to the end of my marriage. I did not even know where to start. There were multiple affairs going on and promises of change and doing the right thing. So, the anger built up after I noticed that he was continuing the same behavior. Just as I got through one situation, something else came along.

I felt that the pain was unbearable at times. However, I believed the Word of the Lord because he said in **1 Corinthians 10:13,**

"There hath no temptation taken you but such as is common to man: but God *is* faithful, who will not suffer you to be tempted above that you are able; but will with the temptation also make a way to escape, that ye may be able to bear *it*" (KJV).

The Word of the Lord also says in **Philippians 4:13, "I can do all *things* through Christ which strengtheneth me" (KJV).** I relied heavily on the Word of God and trusted God at his word. So, the more my husband said and did things that hurt me, the more I prayed and asked God to give me his strength and to heal me.

I continued to take one day at a time and to pray each day. I would go to the altar at church on Sundays and cry out to God. I would get into the presence of God where I did not feel the pain. I prayed and asked the Lord to lift the burden off my heart. I prayed this scripture found in **Matthew 11:28, "Come unto me, all ye that labour and are heavy laden, and I will give you rest" (KJV).**

3. How do you handle the embarrassment?

On one occasion when I was at the courthouse with my ex-husband so that the court could determine child support for his other children and when all the mothers were there, I felt so embarrassed. I prayed that God would give me the strength to stay quiet. I had to do as the scripture stated in **1 Thessalonians 4:11: "And that *ye* study to be quiet, and to do your own *business*, and to work with your own hands, as we commanded you" (KJV).**

I had to hold my piece in this case, and trust God to fight my battle. I did everything I could not to cause a verbal or an emotional outburst. While being in this situation, I felt a lot of strength pulled from me. Remember, I kept to myself, was very quiet, and could not understand why it was happening to me.

I was also embarrassed by the fact that people knew he had

cheated on me. There was so much that went through my mind that I did not know what to process first. So, I prayed for God to strengthen me during the embarrassment and asked God for his help.

Psalm 121 says,

"I will lift up mine eyes unto the hills, from whence cometh my help. My help *cometh* from the LORD, which made heaven and earth. He will not suffer thy foot to be moved: he that keepeth thee will not slumber. Behold, he that keepeth Israel shall neither slumber nor sleep. The LORD *is* thy keeper: the LORD is thy shade upon thy right hand. The sun shall not smite thee by day, nor the moon by night. The LORD shall preserve thee from all evil: he shall preserve thy soul. The LORD shall preserve thy going out and thy coming in from this time forth, and even for evermore" (KJV).

I also wondered who knew about or saw his cheating but did not tell me. I always believed that somewhere somebody knew. However, I found that most people who knew elected to stay quiet to avoid confrontations. This is why having a relationship with Christ is so important. When no one else will tell you, the Lord will reveal what is going on to you.

Luke 12:2 says, "For there is nothing covered, that shall not be revealed; neither hid, that shall not be known" (KJV). When I felt alone because I felt there was no one I could trust enough not to tell others my business, I found that through my constant communication with God that he was on my side.

Matthew 28:20 says, "Teaching them to observe all *things* whatsoever I have commanded you: and, lo, I am with you always, even unto the end of the world. Amen" (KJV).

4. How do you release the anger without wanting to retaliate?

It took quite some time for me to release my hurt, anger, and disappointment with my ex-husband. I said mean things in retaliation but never followed through with them. I remember being at the park and one of his other children's mothers coming and sitting directly in the front of me with her child. How did I handle that? Again, I fought to be quiet because I did not even want her to know I was bothered by the situation. However, it did bother me, and I was angry all over again.

In another case, I remember telling my ex-husband that I was going to shut the power off in the house when he refused to move and had the affair in that house, among other verbal altercations we encountered out of hurt and pain. I found myself getting so angry with him that I just did not like him anymore.

Out of all the years that I had been married to him, I had never been in this place because of all the ongoing lies, betrayal, deceit, and mind manipulation. I almost hated him. Yet I didn't because my mother always taught her children that you did not hate the person but hated the sin that had been committed, which was the work of the devil. Remember **John 10:10, where it says, "The thief cometh not, but for to steal, and to kill, and to destroy: I am come that they might have life, and that they might have it *more* abundantly" (KJV)**. As mentioned in this scripture, the enemy does not care. He wants you to do something to mess up your own life up through your actions of retaliation.

So, at this point, I decided to pray and fast for three days for my heart. I needed God to strengthen and heal my broken heart. There were many nights I cried and was lonely and broken. I just could not understand how someone could vow to love me and then have not only one affair but also continuing multiple affairs as if he was not married.

It was very difficult knowing that other women shared our intimacy. I kept asking myself, *how could this man love me while committing this type of behavior?* Of course, this is not love. In addition to this, one of the women claimed she had gotten my phone number off his phone and had called to make the affair known to me. I guess whenever my ex-husband did not do what she wanted him to do, this was her way of getting back at him. I was somewhat puzzled as to why she wanted to make the affair known to me when she knew all the while that he was married and had a family already. Another possible reason may have been the fact that her desire to be with him increased, so now it was time to let the wife know with hopes of breaking up the marriage.

Trust me. This was a very difficult process. I remained angry and upset for a very long time but knew I had to find a way to get through it. Besides, I had to accept the fact that this was happening because of my husband's actions and not just the other woman's. Here are some scriptures I relied on.

> **"Be ye angry, and sin not: let not the sun go down upon your wrath" (Eph. 4:26 KJV).**

> **"Dearly beloved, avenge not yourselves, but *rather* give place unto wrath: for it is written, Vengeance is mine; I will repay, saith the Lord" (Rom. 12:19 KJV).**

> **"Fret not thyself because of evildoers, neither be thou envious against the workers of iniquity. For they shall soon be cut down like the grass, and wither as the green herb. Trust in the LORD, and do good; so shalt thou dwell in the land, and verily thou shalt be fed. Delight thyself also in the LORD: and he shall give thee the desires of thine heart" (Ps. 37 1–4 KJV).**

I was angry with all parties involved but mainly with my ex-husband for putting himself in a position for this to happen and being a willing participant. He made the vows for better or worse, in sickness and health, and until death do us part. So, I felt that he should have respected his own marriage if no one else did. I was angry with the women because to be honest, I don't' care what a man's status is. He cannot go any further than the woman allows. In these cases, the women understood my husband was married and/or in a long-term relationship with me, yet they did not care.

Therefore, one of them kept the affair quiet until she conceived (twice). After things did no go the way she had planned, she sought to contact me and let me know of her children. Of course, I did not let her know how I truly felt. However, when I got off the phone, my mind could not even gather the thoughts I should deal with first.

In his latest affair, I noticed that while I continued to argue back and forth with him, the more he stayed in this adulterous affair, the more I gave him power over my life, and the more he continued the same lying games. It was not until I decided I was no longer going to let this situation control my life that I realized I was arguing with a demonic spirit that had been operating through him. After blocking him, I asked God to help me with the anger, to remove it from my heart, and to give me his heart. I prayed for my heart!

Two scriptures that helped me were,

> "And he said, Hearken ye, all Judah, and ye inhabitants of Jerusalem, and thou king Jehoshaphat, Thus, saith the LORD unto you, Be not afraid nor dismayed by reason of this great multitude; for the battle *is* not yours, but God's" (2 Chron. 20:15 KJV).

> "Create in me a clean heart, O God; and renew a right spirit within me. Cast me not away from thy presence; and take not thy holy spirit from me" (Ps. 51:10-11 KJV)

5. How do you keep peace with your own children and family members who are angry and watching you suffer?

Through prayer, you can do this because you must do this. I began to talk to my children about what was right when it came to God. At first, I did not tell them because they were very young, and I did not want them to act out. As the kids grew older, they learned of my ex-husband's adulterous acts because they now had other siblings and did not understand where they had come from. However, it was very difficult for me to explain to my youngest son, who was seven years old at the time, because he did not understand what was going on and kept saying he did not want his parents to divorce. In fact, he held onto the marriage up until the age of sixteen, still hoping his father would change and do the right thing so that the family could be united again.

After seeing that his father's behavior never changed, my youngest son finally let go after nine years. Nevertheless, I focused on God because I did not want my kids to go through life with bitterness and anger, making others pay for all that had happened in their lives. So, I kept teaching them the Word of God and most importantly, about forgiveness. Yes, the situation deeply hurt us, but I knew we had to someday forgive and try to let go of the things that had happened.

My scriptures during this time were,

> **"He healeth the broken in heart, and bindeth up their wounds" (Ps. 147:3 KJV).**

> **"The Lord is close to the brokenhearted and saves those who are crushed in spirit "(Ps. 34:18 KJV).**

This brings me to my next question.

6. What do you do about the other children who were conceived from the affairs during your marriage?

Well, I could not even focus on this until I was able to accept, handle, and deal with my own hurt. My husband kept saying that he wanted his marriage and family and claimed to be deeply sorry for his errors. I knew that I still loved him but was deeply hurt, angry, confused, and disappointed with his actions. I wanted him to help me through my pain because I continued to be very sad each day as I tried to make it through. The very thought of knowing that another woman had children or a child by my husband, who had vowed to love me, was a very difficult process.

In one of the affairs that took place while we were dating, another woman's child was conceived. After about five or six years, I began to call the child to try to get to know her. I would seldom put my husband on the phone. This did not work for long because I was not ready and felt disrespected. I left the situation alone for a while.

Being that I had a relationship with the Lord, he would show me things regarding the child. In a dream, I would be walking with her and holding her hand, so I knew that I had to establish a relationship with this child. Again, the children were innocent and had not asked to be there. However, when I saw the children, sometimes it reminded me of the hurt all over again because this did not have to be.

As time went on, every now and then, I would reach out to the child and speak with her on the phone, but I still had some restrictions concerning how this could play out. I knew that I wanted a great level of respect. I decided that whatever happened, I was not going to feel disrespected. I felt that the mother knew my ex-husband was in a long-term relationship. Therefore, I felt she could not disrespect me in any way. I also felt that they would not be allowed to call the shots when it came to the sharing of my space at my house, with my kids, or even with my husband. It was many years before I even allowed her around my children.

Now, this is my testimony. I am not saying this is the right or wrong thing to do but am sharing my experience.

I could not have these children around me at all while I was in a damaged place. It was years before I even tried to allow them to meet my children, who were there siblings. I knew that as a woman of God, I could not allow the anger to sit in my heart, so I continued to pray. However, I could not do any of this without God's strength. I had to seek the face of the Lord to deal with each step. God gave me strength and instructions on how to deal with this situation. My husband did not force this situation on either of these children because he knew I would have left him immediately. I felt as if he knew he could not even bring the matter up.

In this situation, I always reached out to this child even in her teenage years because she began to develop some problems. I reached out to her to check on her, to try to talk to her, and to get her going in the right direction. Of course, there were issues that had developed due to the absence of her father. This situation did not only have a great impact on me as the wife but on everyone else involved.

I truly did not want to be connected to all these people. In addition to this, it was very embarrassing. People began to ask questions because they knew what had happened in the marriage. My children came first, so no one knew of this situation at first.

I was so angry and believe it took me longer to process things because I felt that not only had my ex-husband known he was married but the other woman had known as well, how could they expect me to accept this child or want anything to do with her.

Again, I began to pray and seek God's strength. Through prayer, the Lord began to heal me. No, it was not easy and did not happen overnight. There were times when I saw the mother or the child with the mother when I had to keep my composure. I wondered how someone could be so thoughtless and evil that she didn't even have enough respect for herself to deal with a man who was married.

Nevertheless, I knew I had to get through this. Depending on my ex-husband would not help me get through it. I was too angry and disappointed in him and did not trust anyone. I had to turn to God. I established a life of prayer, reading and studying the Bible, and relying greatly on God. There was no other way for me. I occasionally talked to my mother, who had also experienced this. This gave me some level of comfort, but I was still in a place of hurting. It took time for me to heal, and my husband had to allow me to heal.

Things did not start coming together until the children were grown and on their own because of the level of distrust and the ongoing affairs. This way, he strictly dealt with the children and not their mothers.

On the other hand, as I stated above, this may not be the case for everyone because I feel that if a couple can go through the necessary healing process and respect one another's feelings, in time, this could be worked out and might be able to save their marriage. However, this can't be an ongoing and repeated situation.

7. How do you forgive all the parties involved that have hurt you?

Your healing will be very hard to process completely until you come to a place of forgiving. One of the situations that had me in a bad place was the most recent affair. I kept trying to process the fact that the other woman had called the wife and had demanded that she leave her own husband alone, especially when the wife had not known anything about it.

I wondered if anyone was honoring the commandments of God. Thou shalt not commit adultery. So how could this woman call me and demand that I leave my own husband alone. I couldn't get over the fact that she had seven or eight kids from four different men, none of which were my ex-husband's. So why would my husband get tangled up in something like this when he had multiple kids of his own whom he did not have a relationship with?

When I learned of this affair, just like the others, it did not make any sense at all. I knew I had to let go of the situation because this was not a mistake but was something much greater than that. In addition to this, he was a master liar, I knew that somehow, my kids and I had to get through it.

Developing a relationship with God included knowing what the Word of God said. In this scripture, I found what I had to pray to help me forgive those who had hurt me: **"But if ye forgive not men their trespasses, neither will your Father forgive your trespasses"** (**Matt. 6:15 KJV**), Because I loved God and desired to please him, I asked the Lord to help me forgive those who had hurt me. I asked the Lord to change my heart to his heart so that I could love as he commanded us to love in **John 15:12: "This is my commandment, That ye love one another, as I have loved you"** (**KJV**).

I had to learn how to focus on God and not the problem itself. Yes, the problem still existed, but I had to find my place in God because my hope, reliance, and trust was in him. I knew that if I was going to make it, it was only going to be with the help of the Lord. I had no one else whom I truly felt that I knew or could understand this level of pain that had to be processed. It was all unprocessed and in my mind.

So how did I get through this? It took me eight years to forgive the woman with the two children because she knew he had been in a marriage. When I started ministering, the Lord dealt with me and showed me I needed to tell the woman I forgave her.

So, I telephoned and told her that the Lord had led me to call her. She then told me that she was in the church, had been praying, and knew that this had to be God who had told me to call her because she had been praying. I obeyed the Lord and told the woman that I forgave her. After talking a while, we decided that later down the line, our kids would meet so that they would know who their siblings were. After this, I felt as if a burden had been lifted from me because I wanted to be obedient to the Lord.

However, I still did not allow her to come around my house at all because this was an affair. Therefore, there was still no trust, and a level of respect still had to be maintained. If there were any dealings with the children due to this contact, it would be through me.

In such instances, you must consult God because only God can give you strength to get through something like this. No matter what anyone else says, only God will help you. Not everyone will handle the situation like this, but keep in mind that the other children are innocent.

You see, I can speak on both sides of this because my father was married to another woman. So, I know how it feels to be rejected and unloved at times in this area. As one of the other kids, I could relate to the pain of the wife and would not go around her if my presence bothered her. Before I had been old enough to understand, both my father and his wife had passed away. When I learned how I was conceived, I became angry. There were a lot of questions that remained unanswered due to his passing away. My siblings on my father's side knew of me and accepted me but lost contact with me after my father's passing. This was when I went back to Daytona Beach, Florida, to reside with my mother.

When I moved back to Vero Beach, Florida, my siblings found me through a family member and began interacting with me again. They also introduced me to other family members that knew of me, but I did not know them. Although, they all welcomed me with opened arms, I still felt reserved and uncomfortable in some areas because I was the other child. Despite how I felt, my siblings still treated me kindly and with respect, as if I was no different from the other siblings.

On the other hand, in my situation, I still had to keep on healing, so I kept on praying. Through ongoing communication with the Lord, he led me to a place of fellowship. While going to this place, the Lord began to process the things in me that had happened both spiritually and physically. The Lord began to put my mind, heart, and spirit back together again. He placed me with people that prayed for me and had my best interests at heart. One evangelist respected my space and tried to keep me in a place of happiness by making me laugh. I had to learn how to release myself just to be able to laugh. I found a place where I felt safe to have fun and laugh. Every time I met with this evangelist, I began to have fun and laugh.

On one occasion, she grabbed me and said, "You need to stop being so closed. This is a healing and deliverance ministry, and we are here to help you, not to hurt you. By this time, I broke down crying and stayed in my room. She then told me to come out with the others. We sat on the floor, laughed, and had fun. As she had been going through some jewelry, there had been a bracelet I had really liked. She gave it to me and said I could have it. I got all emotional again as I put it on. I had forgotten how to even receive love from people because of what I had experienced, which made me not trust anybody. She showed me that it was okay.

I also met another evangelist in the ministry who helped me. It took me about a year to open-up and talk with her. She was a counselor. She began to counsel me and pray for me. I knew I was in a depressed place and needed to get all the stuff that was stuck in my head out. I did not know why I would sometimes be sitting there and suddenly the tears would flow. I was very sad and depressed. Moreover, this evangelist began to target the hurting areas in my life and to dig me out of those areas.

In one of our meetings, I opened-up to her about the two other children who had been conceived during my marriage. I also shared about the pain that was caused by different church members telling me that I should not have left my home or my marriage (Yes, as with all the affairs, they still said I should not have left my marriage and continue to say it). I broke down crying again. I had a lot of tension and swelling in my shoulders and neck.

This evangelist grabbed me and began to pray for me because her ministry was in healing and deliverance. As she prayed for my head and began to call out the high blood pressure, strokes, and other things in me, I began to feel some comfort and healing. I began to develop a level of trust with this evangelist. I felt she had my best interests at heart as well when it came to helping me get through my healing and deliverance processes.

She continued to counsel me for another year or so and could see that I was feeling better mentally, emotionally, physically, and spiritually. I was also getting the Word of God, and it fed my spirit and brought nourishment to my mind, body, and soul. I felt I needed to be in this place. I began to thank God for leading me to a place where someone could help me process the pain that I felt no one else could understand. Overall, I thank God for taking care of me and my children, as I healed they were healed as well. No kid wants to see his or her mother suffer but wants to see her happy. I give God all the glory!

8. How do you forgive your husband?

Again, things take time. Even if you live separately, you still need time to heal and process things. You need positive and praying people around you. You do not need people around you who say you should have done this or that or say they would have done or said things differently. You need people who can pray and hear from the Lord with you as it says in **Matthew 18:20: "For where two or three gathered together in my name, there am I in the midst of them" (KJV)**.

I believe that first you must accept the issues at hand. This means accepting that things have occurred so that your healing process can begin, along with fasting and praying. I sought Christian counseling on several occasions. I wanted my ex-husband to repent of his sins and seek God as the Lord and Savior of his life. I wanted him to turn to God, but he had to want this for himself. After I kept hoping and going back and forth with him, his behavior patterns just continued. I started to pray for my heart and asked for the strength to get through it so I could forgive him. I wanted to obey God. I did not want to be bitter and angry all of my life. I wanted to forgive. So, I started seeking God and relying on his word, which says in **Psalm 147:3, "He healeth the broken in heart, and bindeth up their wounds" (KJV). Psalm 34:18 says, "The Lord *is* nigh unto them that are of a broken heart; and saveth such as be of a contrite spirit" (KJV).**

I often told him that I forgave him and really thought I had. Yet when certain things occurred, I was angry with him all over again. I could not forgive him when he continued to frustrate me and to say things that made me more bitter. So, I told him that I forgave him for all he had done to me and that I was sorry if I had offended him in any way because I wanted my heart to be right with God and to be free from all hurt and pain.

After this, I stopped talking to him as much as possible. I felt I had talked, prayed, ministered, hoped, and done all that I knew how to do. Now I relied on the Lord, as he said in **1 Peter 5:7: "Casting all your care upon him; for he careth for you" (KJV).**

You see, I let go of the thought that the other woman had won my ex-husband from me. In all actuality, it was not even about that because if I wanted him, I could have him at any time. I just refused to have him in the condition he was in and to allow myself to be disrespected. I felt and knew I deserved better than that. If this type of person had no respect for herself, then so be it. I left it all in God's hands and relied solely on God. At this point, I just wanted God. Eventually, I did forgive my ex-husband, told him that I hoped he would find happiness, and wished him well. Occasionally, I also prayed for him.

9. How do you accept that the relationship is over?

Based on my experience, once I knew that I had done all that I could do, including praying, fasting, trying, hoping, ministering, etc., and there was still no change, I knew that it was over. I knew that I could not spend any more years in the same situation. I just wanted to live and be happy. He wanted to remain in the marriage with me but did not want to change or turn to God for help. I began to look at everything around me and really seek God ... I mean really seek God. Then I had to *decide* and take control of my own life.

After twenty-nine years, I decided that I was not going through another year of a repeat cycle of his adultery, lies, and betrayal. I really wanted to be happy, so I told him that I wouldn't do it another year and that this was his last opportunity to decide to straighten up and do the right thing. Yet he continued to lie and deny the affairs while the Lord showed me otherwise. So, I took control of my life and *decided* this situation was not going to control me. I took the necessary measures to begin moving forward by cutting down my communication with him, praying, and asking God to break all soul ties and to strengthen me to move forward in him.

I took it one day at a time. There were times when I still wanted to call my ex-husband, but I prayed or started doing something else to keep moving forward. At that point in my life, I learned to be happy with the peace the Lord had allowed my kids and me to have in our own private space. So, I *decided* to leave the past behind and to do the things that would move me forward into my future.

10. How do you get back up and move forward?

Once I *decided* that it was over, I took control of my life. Instead of allowing him to keep saying how he was going to fix things and do things, I began to tell him I was not going through another year like I had been. I told him, "What benefit is it to stay married to you when you are still involved with an affair? No, I am not going through another year like this." You see, I *decided*. I *took control of my own life*! He no longer was allowed to have a say in my life, which had really only left me in a delayed place. I decided to move forward in what the Lord told me to do, such as writing this book.

I hope this book will heal, set free, and deliver someone out of that broken and disappointed place. Just as the Lord saved, delivered, helped, comforted, strengthened, encouraged me, prayed for me, and gave me peace, it is my prayer for you as well that you may find a place of peace and a heart to love the true and living God as Lord of your life and ruler of your heart, mind, soul, and spirit. The Lord says in **Isaiah 26:3, "Thou wilt keep *him* in perfect peace, *whose* mind *is* stayed on *thee*: because he trusted in thee"** (KJV).

May God, bless you,
Prophetess Ruth Gold

CHAPTER 11

Points to Remember

N ow that I have gone through my process of deliverance regarding the issues in my previous marriage, I have come to recognize the patterns and spirits that operated and held me in captivity at that time. From the beginning, there were lies and deceit that continued throughout our dating period and our marriage. I am writing this book, hoping to encourage young ladies and men to recognize the spirits that operate in other individuals before they continue into relationships. In addition, I would like to help men and women understand what happens spiritually when they go out and have affairs.

One of the points I would like to make is that you should never move in with a man or woman if you are not married to that person. This is mainly because you are disobeying the commandments of God, especially if the relationship leads to fornication. Therefore, without repentance, you will eventually suffer the consequences of this sin. The Bible tells us that disobedience is as the sin of witchcraft. **1 Samuel 15:23 says, "For rebellion *is* as the sin of witchcraft, and stubbornness *is* as iniquity and idolatry. Because thou has rejected the word of the Lord, he hath also rejected thee from *being* king" (KJV).**

You see here that the Lord sent Samuel to anoint Saul as king over Israel. Saul was then given instructions by God to destroy the Amalekites for attacking Israel as they were coming into the Promised

Land. Saul was told to destroy all the Amalekites and not to spare them. However, Saul did not do as the Lord had commanded. He destroyed what he felt was worthless and kept the king and what he considered were the best of things. Basically, Saul did what he wanted to do. You see, this was not what the Lord told him to do. Because of his disobedience to God, he was rejected as king. Not only was he rejected but he built a monument for himself (*See* 1 Samuel 15:12 KJV). He also lied to Samuel about the battle, stating that he had performed the commandments of the Lord (*See* 1 Samuel 15:13 KJV). Therefore, his rebellion was noted as the sin of witchcraft.

As I continued to pray, I realized that through disobedience, rebellion, and adultery, this was more than just affairs. This was *witchcraft*, which included mind-manipulating and seducing spirits, which we will discuss further in Chapter 12.

Also know that only God has the power to change an individual, so fasting and prayer is what leads to change. I hoped, prayed, and tried different things in my own way, but when I got to a place where I felt I had done everything possible, I let go and left the situation in God's hands, which were the best hands.

If you are married and one of you should fall into a backslidden place, remember that you must continue to fast and pray because Scripture says,

> **"Then he saith, I will return into my house from whence I came out; and when he is come, he findeth *it* empty; swept, and garnished. Then goeth he, and taketh with himself seven other spirits more wicked than himself, and they enter in and dwell there; and the last *state* of that man is worse than the first. *Even* so shall it be also unto this wicked generation" (Matt. 12:44–45 KJV).**

Another scripture says, **"For it had been better for them not to have known the way of righteousness, than after they have**

known it, to turn from the holy commandment delivered unto them" (2 Peter 2:21 KJV).

So now you are dealing with even more spirits than you started with, which requires a great deal of fasting and prayer as well as deliverance. I would also suggest seeking some spiritual counseling as well as having a spiritual leader pray with you.

Any sin, of course, leads to consequences. In this case, ongoing multiple sexual affairs not only led to separation in the marriage but more importantly, separation from God. There were also mental attacks against the entire family.

Let's look at these two scriptures:

"Thou shalt not commit adultery" (Exodus 20: 14).

"Flee fornication. Every sin that a man doeth is without the body; but he that committeth fornication sinneth against his own body" (1 Corinthians 6:18 KJV).

These two seem to be the most committed sins across the globe. Some people choose to move in with each other without getting married as if they were husband and wife. Because many people do not want to wait and do it God's way, they are led by the flesh and choose their way for various reasons. However, is this way the right way when it comes to the commandments of God? What happened to the fear of God? What will happen to the soul if a person's time should come?

There were many examples in the Old Testament of what happened because of the spirit of seduction and lust. Some examples were King David with Bathsheba (*See* 2 Samuel 11:1–4), King Solomon (*See* 1 Kings 11:1–6), Joseph (*See* Genesis 39:6–12), and Samson (*See* Judges 16: 1), just to name a few. Nothing good came out of this.

Because this was my first and only serious relationship, I made many errors. As I became intimate with my ex-husband, I also became more emotionally, physically, and spiritually attached to him. I was so in love until I put him before myself, which was the wrong thing to do. Because of all that I had endured, I had to find me again. I lost who I was in this relationship/marriage. I was focused on doing all that I could to keep the marriage and did not realize that no matter what I did, things would get better for a little while but then would go back to the way they were before. It took a very long process for me to find who I was again. I had to learn how to live again.

The first thing I did was make sure I stayed in prayer and communication with God. If I was going to get through this, I knew the only way was going to be with God. I stayed continually before God so that I could be led by him. I decided to stop going to others for their opinions and focused on God.

Secondly, I was in a church that was totally against divorce. They truly believed that a person should stay in a marriage regardless of the situation unless one spouse died. Nevertheless, I had to put this behind me and seek God for my own answer because I had been unhappy for many years. I came to realize that this was my life and that my situation needed peace.

John 10:10 says, "The thief cometh, not, but for to steal, and to kill, and destroy: I am come that they might have life, and that they might have it more abundantly" (KJV). In this scripture, the enemy comes to take from our lives, but Jesus gives us life so that we can have peace, love, and joy.

Yes, we make decisions, and sometimes they may not be the right decisions. However, the Word of the Lord says in 1 John 1:9, "If we confess our sins, he is faithful and just to forgive us *our* sins, and to cleanse us from all unrighteousness" (KJV). So, when we admit that we have done wrong, our Lord will forgive us and clean us from our sins. However, we should not intentionally, repeatedly, or knowingly sin.

I believe that the Lord will help us so we are not stuck in any situation. I felt stuck in my unhealthy marriage. I felt I had no way out. I did not know how to get out because my mind was in a confused, distraught, and terrible place. I could not think straight or remember anything. I had to drop out of school because I could not retain information.

How did I survive this attack on my mind? I did not understand what was happening to me spiritually. So, I sought counseling before I left my home altogether, and it did not seem to help. I was losing my mind and knew I had to get help. I knew I deserved better but for some reason, I could not make up my mind to leave.

So, I began to seek God's face, and the Lord began to reveal his directions and instructions to me. The Lord began to connect me with people as he showed me who my connection would be with. He also dealt with the person as to their connection with me. It was time for me to hear, obey, and follow God.

One of the other problems that I struggled with was feeling like the other woman had won and had taken my husband. Even though I knew this was not the case, my ex-husband made her think this was the case because he played these back-and-forth games while lying to both sides.

When I prayed, and decided to take charge of my own life, it did not matter what she thought, said, or did. My focus became God, and he was the one I trusted and relied on. I decided I no longer wanted to be a part of this type of mind manipulation and control. I needed healing and deliverance in my mind, heart, soul, and spirit, so I decided to seek God like never before.

It is sad that some men and women in this world today have no respect for their marriage vows, as well as some women not having a problem dating married men or breaking up homes. My question is, what happened to women who respect themselves? Where are the true standards for what is right when it comes to the commandments of God? Why is it that some people no longer fear the Lord?

Scripture says, **"And unto man he said, Behold, the fear of the Lord, that is wisdom; and to depart from evil is understanding"**

(Job 28:28 KJV). Another scripture says, "**The fear of the Lord is the beginning of knowledge: *but* fools despise wisdom and instruction**" (Prov. 1:7 KJV).

It appears that some women in cases like this have apparently become so desperate that they do not mind sharing a man or just want a piece of a man. When speaking with different women, I asked them why they thought women got involved with married men or wanted to fight over men who were in long-term relationships. Women get involved with married men for several reasons. Here are some of their responses:

1. A woman hopes that he will leave his home for her.
2. A woman does not want to be in a committed relationship but wants sex.
3. When money is involved, a woman purposely becomes pregnant so she can blackmail the man. She does not care for herself or anyone else.
4. A woman might have had this happen to her and has taken on a spirit of retaliation.

The bottom line is that this type of behavior is wrong according to the Word of God. Even though excuses are often made for affairs, we must ask ourselves, if we were standing before God, would this excuse be pleasing to our Lord? The main concern should be the fear of what the Lord will do to us if we disobey his commandments.

On the other hand, let's look at the right way of doing things. One of the examples in the Bible is in the book of Ruth (KJV). Some of us know the story. When Ruth's (the Moabite) husband died, she decided to go with her mother-in-law Naomi to her people in Judah. Ruth decided that she wanted to serve the same God that Naomi served. As a result, they went on to Bethlehem at the start of the harvest time.

While gleaning, she met Boaz. When she went to present herself to Boaz, she did it in a respectful manner. Ruth did as her mother-in-law had told her to do so that she would be prepared for this man of God. She washed and anointed herself, put on her best garments, and went down to the threshing floor. She did not make herself known to the man while he was eating and drinking.

In our world today, I have known women to dress inappropriately and to go to clubs, churches, and events looking for any man. The seducing spirit on this woman is loud, along with her appearance. Men with the same spirit will look at her. She attracts men according to her appearance and spirit.

Ruth did not go and try to seduce Boaz by wearing apparel with her cleavage showing or with a very short dress or skirt that looked as though it had been painted on her. She prepared for the man of God. The Bible says she uncovered his feet and lay down there. She presented herself as a woman of respect, and Boaz treated her as a woman of respect.

Another example was in the book of Esther. When Esther needed to see the king on behalf of her people, she prepared herself. Scripture says in **Esther 5: 1, "Now it came to pass on the third day, that Esther put on her royal apparel, and stood in the inner court of the king's house, over against the king's house: and the king sat upon his royal throne in the royal house, over against the gate of the house" (KJV).**

Again, she did not come in there all loud and dressed wrong. She presented herself in a quiet manner and dressed in her royal robe. The king noticed her, and she found favor in his sight. So, what I am saying is that you do not have to dress revealing to get the right man's attention. Again, I said the *right* man and not any kind of man, especially not a married man.

Let's look at **Hebrews 13:4 about this. "Marriage is honorable in all, and the bed undefiled: but whoremongers and adulterers God will judge." Matthews 5:27–30 says, "Ye have heard that it was said by them of old time, Thou shalt not commit adultery: But I say unto you, That whosoever looketh on a woman to lust**

after her hath committed adultery with her already in his heart"
(KJV).

So, my question is, why have some people become so comfortable
in disobeying the Word of God? Another scripture to take note of
is **1 Corinthians 7:1–3, which says, "Now concerning the things
whereof ye wrote unto me: It is good for a man not to touch a
woman. Nevertheless, to avoid fornication, let every woman
have her own husband. Let the husband render unto the wife
due benevolence: and likewise also the wife unto the husband"
(KJV).** You see, the Word of God does not say anything about
sharing a man. Again, the scripture says let each one have their own.

CHAPTER 12

Soul Ties

Not only was I physically tied in this, I was emotionally, mentally, and spiritually tied in this. How can these unhealthy soul ties be broken?

1. Mind=Mental connection
2. Heart=Emotional connection
3. Soul=Physical connection
4. Spirit=Sexual connection

I was physically and sexually tied because I could not get my mind to leave my ex-husband. After all these years, I was physically tied. I was also sexually tied because he had been my husband. When we were together, this created a deep-rooted soul tie spiritually and emotionally. All these ties had to be broken for me to be free in my mind, heart, soul, and spirit.

Let's talk about the physical tie. I figured I would start here because I left physically first. When I got to the point where I just did not know what to do, I kept praying, fasting, reading the Word of God, and going to church. Then God began to show me the woman of God. I did not know why I was seeing her, but he kept showing her to me.

Eventually, I started going to church as the Lord led me to

another ministry in another state. I started going once a month, increased this to twice a month, and then went almost every week. I did this for a couple of months and eventually moved to this state. I decided I could not take anymore and sought peace for myself and my children.

Although I had separated physically from this relationship, I remained tied in the other three areas. As a result, I still went back every so often to my home in Florida, and we continued in the relationship. He also continued to come to the state I had moved to every two weeks. Even though I had moved, we still had these ties. We continued doing this for another three years or so.

After I learned of his other affairs, I ceased the sexual and physical parts of the marriage, and upon his visits, I required him to get a hotel. It took me another two years to break free from the emotional aspect of this, which consisted of crying, worrying, and calling.

The most difficult tie to break was the mental tie because my mind had been so attacked. In other words, I did not know I was under a witchcraft attack. I underwent a massive amount of mental confusion. I could not understand what was going on in my mind. All I knew was that I suddenly could not retain information. When I would read, I could not comprehend it. It was almost as if my mind had to be trained all over again how to function. I did not know what had happened to me, but I knew something had.

One of my spiritual leaders mentioned witchcraft. So, I began to study the signs and symptoms of a person under a witchcraft attack. While reading the article *5 Clear Signs Witchcraft Is Attacking You Right Now*. I noticed that I experienced the symptoms noted in the article: I had trouble paying attention and felt as if my mind had been scrambled like an egg. I also had problems focusing, my mind wandered, and I overanalyzed everything as if my mind was constantly racing until it became tired. I felt like I had run a marathon in my mind. I also experienced fatigue, depression, and other health problems.

In addition to this article, I purchased a book by Jonas Clark titled *Exposing Spiritual Witchcraft*, which showed some of the characteristics of witchcraft that I had experienced, including mental confusion, mind manipulation, problems with attention and comprehension, and feeling unbalanced. It was as if I had to constantly fight to remember and pay attention. These resources were very helpful with understanding the spirit of witchcraft.

Nevertheless, once I began to realize what was going on in me, I became hurt, angry, and confused. Words could not explain how I felt. I kept saying that I never bothered anyone and would not do such a thing to hurt anyone else, so why would someone want to do this to me? I just knew I wanted to be free from this, so I began to seek God, fast, and pray. I wanted my deliverance from this. I wanted peace, joy, and my mind back. I wanted *me* back. I had clearly lost track of me. Most of all, I wanted the freedom to read the Word of God without my mind wandering and to worship and praise the Lord without feeling that I had lost something right after I had received impartation.

I thank God for placing me in a healing and deliverance ministry around people I met who were experienced and gifted in this area and knew how to fast and pray for my deliverance. It was as if my mind, body, soul, and spirit had to be put back together again because everything was out of alignment.

Nevertheless, I began to cry out for God's help in this. I wanted to be made whole again, so I fasted and prayed for the Lord to take my ex-husband off my heart, mind, soul, and spirit. I began to pray and ask God to break all unhealthy and ungodly soul ties. I kept praying, and as he continued his affairs, I kept getting stronger and stronger. Things that had bothered me from his actions before no longer bothered me. However, getting my mind free was the longest process.

I am still trying to recover from such an attack. I tell you that only God could free me from this. I joined a healing and deliverance ministry that interceded and prayed for me. I had to fight and be consistent in praying and believing what the Lord said in his Word about my mind. I also had to be consistent in reading his Word while fasting, praying, and pleading the blood of Jesus over my life because it was hard to break this in the natural world. However, there is nothing too hard for the Lord.

My final breakthrough came when I sold my house in Florida. I then pursued filing my divorce. Once all of this had been settled and done, I felt I had nothing holding or tying me to my past. I thank God for my peace and my freedom today. Now I take time out for me and my children while enjoying me because I found me and am happy.

Our Prayer

Father God, we thank you, heavenly Father, for your grace and mercy. Lord, we thank you for your love and kindness. Lord, we thank you for your patience with us and because you are Lord of lords and King of kings. Heavenly Father, we ask that you look on the people who are reading this book. We ask that you encourage and strengthen them in whatever they may be facing even now. Heavenly Father, let them know that you are right here to help those who are drawing near to you and asking for your help. Lord, we ask that readers will find a deeper relationship with you as Lord of their lives and Ruler of their hearts, minds, souls, and spirits and that you would give them a peace that surpasses all understanding. Lord, we ask that you would break them free from any strongholds, yokes, or bondages in which they feel captive, for Lord God, you said in your Word that you came to set the captive free and whom the Son sets free is free indeed.

In Jesus's name, we pray. Amen!

NOTES

Clark, J. (1995), **Exposing Spiritual Witchcraft.** Hallandale Beach, Florida: Spirit of Life Publishing.

LeClair, J. (2015, October 8). **5 Clear Signs Witchcraft Is Attacking You Right Now.** Retrieved from URL (https://www. charismamag.com/blogs/the-plumb-line/24566-5-clear-signs-witchcraft-is-attacking-you-right-now).

Printed in the United States
By Bookmasters